Critical Guides to Spanish Texts

45   Rulfo: El llano en llamas

Critical Guides to Spanish Texts

EDITED BY J.E. VAREY AND A.D. DEYERMOND

RULFO

El llano en llamas

William Rowe

Lecturer in Spanish-American Literature
King's College, London

Grant & Cutler Ltd *in association with*
Tamesis Books Ltd 1987

© Grant & Cutler Ltd
1987

Library of Congress Cataloging-in-Publication Data

Rowe, William.
    Rulfo, el llano en llamas.

    (Critical guides to Spanish texts; 45)
    Bibliography: p.
    1. Rulfo, Juan—Criticism and interpretation.
I. Title. II. Series
PQ7297.R89Z883 1987   863   87-21078
ISBN 0-7293-0267-9 (pbk.)

ISBN 0-7293-0267-9

I.S.B.N. 84-599-2119-0

DEPÓSITO LEGAL: V. 2.168 - 1987

Printed in Spain by
Artes Gráficas Soler, S.A., Valencia
for
GRANT & CUTLER LTD
55-57, GREAT MARLBOROUGH STREET, LONDON W1V 2AY
and
27, SOUTH MAIN STREET, WOLFEBORO, NH 03894-2069, USA

Contents

For Angie and Julie

Preface

Juan Rulfo (1918-1986) is undoubtedly one of the great Spanish-American writers of this century. He is best known for the novel *Pedro Páramo*, but *El llano en llamas* is also, in its own different way, a masterpiece. It is perhaps more difficult to define the mastery of the stories of *El llano*. Their extraordinary depth is not necessarily apparent at first reading, but they still communicate new aspects after many readings. The major critics have tended to concentrate their attention on Rulfo's novel, though Angel Rama entitles his essay 'una primera lectura' (*15*), suggesting that a great deal more remains to be said about the short stories. It is hoped that the present study will contribute to the wider recognition of the importance of Rulfo's stories.

This is not the occasion to assess the place of Rulfo in Spanish-American literature. However, an indication of his importance can be given by mentioning some key responses. One of these is the early enthusiasm of the Peruvian novelist José María Arguedas who was concerned, like Rulfo, with communicating a popular oral culture to his readers.[1] By the late 1960s, Rulfo was recognized as a pioneer of the renaissance of the Latin-American novel, then called the 'boom' (*8, 20*). García Márquez stressed that without reading Rulfo he could not have written *Cien años de soledad*. More recently, Rama and Roa Bastos have taken up Arguedas's insight, drawing attention to the transculturative qualities of Rulfo's work, i.e. to the fact that it takes its materials and its language from a marginal oral culture and not from the dominant Western-style culture (*15, 25, 26*).

I have not attempted an exhaustive commentary on all of the stories in the volume, although I have aimed to tackle the most difficult or notable, on the assumption that others, such as

---

[1] José María Arguedas, 'Reflexiones peruanas sobre un narrador mexicano', *El Comercio*, Suplemento Dominical (8 May 1960), p.3.

'Anacleto Morones', should not present the reader with any difficulties outside those already discussed. My method has been to include in each chapter one or two stories which exemplify a particular aspect of the book as a whole and in each case to offer a workable interpretation. Thus although the discussion of time is largely confined to 'Díles que no me maten', the ideas developed are intended to be useful for reading all the other stories. Some of the concepts it was found necessary to use, particularly in connection with the irrational and with language, derive from fairly complex theories. I have aimed to avoid any obscurity or unnecessary difficulty and have made clear what my sources are.

Quotations from *El llano en llamas* are from the most readily available edition, that published by Cátedra (Madrid, 1985); this is based on the 1982 Mexican edition (Fondo de Cultura Económica) which was corrected by Rulfo, and has the advantage of including notes on Mexicanisms. References to items in the Bibliographical Note are indicated by an italic numeral in parentheses, followed where necessary by a page number, thus: (*15*, p.3).

An earlier version of Chapter 4 of this study was published in *Cuadernos Hispanoamericanos*, No. 421-23 (July-September 1985).

1. Reading Rulfo

Works of literature which break existing conventions require from the reader a particular attentiveness. Subsequently these new demands on the reader are codified by critics and given labels such as 'the post-Joycean novel'. Rulfo was one of the first writers in Latin America to thoroughly break up traditional narrative structures, and his work requires that the reader recognize the kind of techniques being used. But rather than entering into a discussion of Rulfo's techniques in themselves, it will be more useful to examine what is needed if our reading of *El llano en llamas* is to succeed in engaging adequately with the stories. Therefore in this introductory chapter I give a close reading of two of the stories; much of what is found in them, particularly as regards the position of the reader, is relevant to all the other stories.

What the reader is told in Rulfo's stories is limited almost entirely to what the characters are aware of. But in order to grasp the full meaning of a story, the reader has to go beyond the characters' view of their world. The incompleteness and partiality of the characters' perceptions, the general atmosphere of obscurity, invites in the reader an urge to complete and explain. We thus become involved in constructing a fuller picture out of limited information. This means working out what is happening, rather than taking it at face value; but, in order to do so, we have to go through two stages. Firstly, since everything is filtered through the characters, we have to learn to look through their eyes, which means finding out how their consciousness works and getting inside it. By recognizing the limits of their awareness we reach the second stage, which is where we go beyond their consciousness and look back at it. Put simply, this means we move from looking through the characters to looking at them.

'Macario', although not the first story in the volume to be

written, is the best introduction to Rulfo's stories because it
dramatizes how we are required to look through a character's
eyes. Macario the character is the first-person narrator of the
story, and what he says is all we have to go on. The idea of
putting the 'seeing eye' inside the story, as an internal narrator,
is a standard device of modern fiction. Henry James, who in his
own fiction as well as in his critical essays gave special priority to
this technique, considered that the internal viewer of events
should be the most polished of possible mirrors — one which
would show the events of the story to the reader as clearly as
possible.[2] What would happen if the mirror were an unreliable,
distorting one? In this case the reader has to assess the nature of
events, but can do so only by recognizing the ways in which the
mirror distorts, i.e. by understanding how the character's mind
works.

Macario's monologue takes place while he sits waiting to kill
the frogs which might wake up his 'godmother'. His relationship
with the *madrina* (which in this case is probably a polite word
for foster-mother) is not clear and is something we have to work
out. All that we have to go on is what passes through his mind.
For instance the words 'Mi madrina también dice eso' (p.87) are
his first mention of her: but the *también* indicates that she was
already in his thoughts. A little later he says, 'También los ojos
de mi madrina son negros', associating her with the blackness of
toads, and toads are what you are not supposed to eat and therefore bad. We put these together with other details: that she gives
him the leftovers to eat, that he will not question what she says
although it does not inspire belief in him. The picture we get is
one of tabooed hostility on his part: the morality he has learnt
will not allow him to show his anger against her.

He has been told that he tried to strangle someone:

Un día inventaron que yo andaba ahorcando a alguien;
que le apreté el pescuezo a una señora nada más por
nomás. Yo no me acuerdo. Pero, a todo esto, es mi

[2] Henry James, 'Preface to *The Golden Bowl*', in *The Art of the Novel*
(London: Scribners, 1935), pp.327-48 (pp.327-28).

madrina la que dice lo que yo hago y ella nunca anda con
mentiras. (p.88)

Not to remember something as important as that is extraordinary; so also is the idea that someone else must be right
about you even though you do not remember: this is one of
several occasions where his mentality collides with ours. The
notion of an objective reality breaks down. How far can we or
should we supply the missing objectivity? For instance, there is a
sense in which the woman in the street, as object of Macario's
anger, must be a substitute for the *madrina*. Nevertheless, this is
not what we are told, since Rulfo keeps us inside Macario's way
of looking at things. Macario does not conceptualize his
experiences; in fact he does not even take that first step towards
rationality which is naming things: for him, Felipa's breasts are
'los bultos esos que ella tiene donde tenemos solamente las
costillas' (p.88).

Throughout, there is a lack of explanation. This is particularly
so with Macario's hunger. The madness that other people
attribute to him is their attempt to explain his incessant hunger.
But the result is to take away the meaning of his hunger, by
imposing conventional social attitudes. Macario's language is
the language of desire, as against the objectifying language of
social control. Two kinds of logic are going on in the story, the
logic of Macario's hunger and conventional social logic: thus
Macario eats the frogs, 'aunque no se coman'. For him Felipa's
milk is like the milk of paradise, the only thing that fills his
hunger and relieves his obsession with hell. The absence of
explanation permits the story to open up a deep and disturbing
level of reality, which cannot be resolved by conventional social
morality and which one might call primitive, provided that word
does not suggest an attitude of superiority. On this level, the
meaning of his hunger derives from a loss which cannot be
filled: the loss of the mother, and particularly of the mother's
milk and all that this represents. This loss, which connects with
Rulfo's biography (see Chapter 2, below) is a theme which
occurs in several Rulfo stories and which is always associated
with a violent response on the part of the person who suffers it.

Macario's violence is directed more against himself than
against others:

> Uno da de topes contra los pilares del corredor horas
> enteras y la cabeza no se hace nada, aguanta sin quebrarse.
> Y uno da de topes contra el suelo; primero despacito,
> después más recio y aquello suena como un tambor. Igual
> que el tambor que anda con la chirimía, cuando viene la
> chirimía a la función del Señor ... Y mi madrina dice que si
> en mi cuarto hay chinches y cucarachas y alacranes es
> porque me voy a ir a arder en el infierno si sigo con mis
> mañas de pegarle al suelo con mi cabeza. Pero lo que yo
> quiero es oír el tambor. Eso es lo que ella debería saber.
> Oírlo, como cuando uno está en la iglesia, esperando salir
> pronto a la calle para ver cómo es que aquel tambor se oye
> de tan lejos, hasta lo hondo de la iglesia y por encima de las
> condenaciones del señor cura. (pp.89-90)

This violence is first of all a way of being, both a substitute for
the tenderness he lacks and a basic violence which is the everyday truth of his life in that it expresses his relationship with the
environment. The banging of his head on the ground also
reminds him of the sound of the drum which when heard in
church blots out the priest's message of sin and death, just as
later on he says he will not kill the crickets because their chirping
keeps away the sound of the souls in torment. On this basis we
can work out that his head-banging is a way of blotting out of
his consciousness that fear of hell which haunts him.

How can we respond to his strange use of the word *uno*? It
suggests that he looks on himself as another person: there is a
part of himself which is alien to him, like an object, and which
cannot be reconciled with the 'yo'. This 'uno' is others' judge-
ment of him, the identity which society seeks to impose on him
and which he refuses: as the 'uno' he refuses to answer others'
accusations or even to speak, using his head only to make the
sound of a drum. When he speaks, he is 'yo', a person for himself, who exists in terms of his hunger. The reader's urge to put
an age to him, or to see him as backward, arises from his dis-

turbingly uncontrolled behaviour. For instance, his sexual attitude to Felipa mixes the feelings of an infant with those of an adolescent boy. But if we find Macario childish, against what are we measuring him? What would 'growing up' consist of? Rulfo does not in fact allow us to attribute a definite age to him and he challenges and subverts our categories of thinking. To assess his age (e.g. 'a mental age of seven') or to label him as mad are attempts to fit him into our world, by controlling him and putting him inside safe boundaries, whereas Macario in fact resists the rationality which adults seek to impose on children, and by the same token the story confronts the reader with the fact that our own rationality might be distorting and repressive. Thus the process of reading reaches a point where our need to explain is confronted with the fact that this might involve imposing social categories which would explain away and betray the experiences portrayed.

Therefore there are limits to how far we can carry through the move from looking through Macario to looking at him. The categories we bring to bear, drawn from social rules and standards, tend to clash with a person who has resisted social moulding. Critics have tended to rationalize the story, for instance by labelling Macario 'un niño retardado', who suffers from some 'defecto mental' (*10*, p.107), safely isolating him from us and diminishing the capacity of the text to disturb us, when in fact the story speaks to the child in everyone. On a more general level, there has been a tendency to explain the behaviour of Rulfo's characters as deriving from their cultural limitations as peasants. Again, the result is to keep the text at a distance and to prevent it challenging the way we think about reality. The importance of 'Macario' for our reading of the book as a whole is that the boy goes further in verbalizing the primitive, non-rational level, which in other stories is more implicit.

If 'Macario' lacks a sharp visual outline, this is no less true of 'No oyes ladrar los perros', a story which takes place at night. In an interview with Joseph Sommers, Rulfo describes his absorption as an adolescent with the misty Nordic world of writers like Knut Hamsun: 'un mundo brumoso ... que ... me sustrajo de esta situación tan luminosa donde vivimos nosotros'

(*28*, p.17). By bringing a dimension of darkness to the glare of
the Mexican landscape, Rulfo's writing creates a space in which
more obscure levels of reality can express themselves. In
'Macario' this has to do with loss of the mother; in 'No oyes',
with another fundamental Rulfo theme: the relationship
between father and son.

The hazy outline of things in 'No oyes' makes it quite the
opposite of photographic in its method of engaging the reader.
The clearest scene is the first, but even this is illuminated not by
the differentiating light of day but by the light of the moon,
which tends to merge what it touches, here turning the two men
into a single shape:

> La sombra larga y negra de los hombres siguió
> moviéndose de arriba abajo, trepándose a las piedras,
> disminuyendo y creciendo según avanzaba por la orilla del
> arroyo. Era una sola sombra, tambaleante.
> La luna venía saliendo de la tierra, como una llamarada
> redonda. (p.146)

The picture is incomplete, but this involves us, making us want
to know more and engaging our imagination. The single
stumbling shadow made by the two men in the moonlight is
grotesque and disquieting, not least because it seems to have a
life of its own: we are led to experience the shadow itself — the
dark side of the two men's relationship — as the protagonist of
the story. Rulfo illuminates the scene only partially, making just
a few details stand out from the surrounding darkness. As we
read on, we gradually put together a wider sense of what is
occurring. The two men are father and son. The son, who is a
thief, has been badly wounded, and the father is carrying him on
his back to a village where there is a doctor. It is the middle part
of the story which sheds this light on the situation. As Angel
Rama points out in his profoundly perceptive essay on this
story, 'la atmósfera iluminada ... corresponde a la racional-
ización (por introducirse de lleno en la eticidad)' (*15*, p.3); i.e.
this stage of the story brings in a moral dimension, previously
absent, showing us the two men as father and son (not just

'hombres'), tied to each other by certain moral obligations. Nevertheless, the first dark, amoral image remains, to be reactivated by the ending. There also remains the question of why the father cannot see or hear, its full meaning to be released, again, only at the end.

Given that this is a story about powerful emotions, it is appropriate to consider how Rulfo conveys the father's emotion. In the passage that follows, it is the son who speaks first:

> —Tengo mucha sed y mucho sueño.
> —Me acuerdo cuando naciste. Así eras entonces. Despertabas con hambre y comías para volver a dormirte. Y tu madre te daba agua, porque ya te habías acabado la leche de ella. No tenías llenadero. Y eras muy rabioso. Nunca pensé que con el tiempo se te fuera a subir aquella rabia a la cabeza ... Pero así fue. Tu madre, que descanse en paz, quería que te criaras fuerte. Creía que cuando tú crecieras irías a ser su sostén. No te tuvo más que a ti. El otro hijo que iba a tener la mató. Y tú la hubieras matado otra vez si ella estuviera viva a estas alturas. (p.149)

What is the connection between the present moment (when the father has the son on his back) and the past remembered by the father? Rulfo does not explain, but we can find the link if we enter the father's mind and follow the way his thinking works. What we are seeing is the father's anger against the son. He feels that the son killed the mother: wanting too much milk as a baby is something he associates with her death when pregnant for the second time — in the father's mind, the unborn child that caused the death of the mother represents the son now on his back. These are the causes of the father's impotent rage. There is also, in his thinking, a connection between the son's present violence as a thief and his hunger as a child. This recalls the theme, in 'Macario', of the child's thwarted desire for the mother's milk, and its connection with violence. Being angry with a small child because it is hungry is a morally tabooed anger, just as is the father's rage at his wounded son. On a deeper level, the father is angry with the son both for being born and for dying — not so much for anything he has done (such as the thieving and murdering) but for being there at all. Also pressing on the father's consciousness is the son's lack of love for him: the reference he makes earlier to the son's killing his godfather (whose name, Tranquilino, adds to the grotesque humour of the story) hints at a sense in which the father feels that the son is killing him — a notion which is also suggested in the vice-like grip of the son's hands around the father's head.

With short stories, more than with novels, re-reading is a special aspect of the reader's relationship to the text. The full meaning of a story often comes when, having reached the end, we go back over it in our minds. Just before the end the father feels the son loosen his grip:

> le pareció que la cabeza, allá arriba, se sacudía como si sollozara.
>
> Sobre su cabello sintió que caían gruesas gotas, como de lágrimas.
>
> —¿Lloras, Ignacio? Lo hace llorar a usted el recuerdo de su madre, ¿verdad? (p.149)

We do not know whether these are tears, or drops of blood — the son does not speak again. We do not know because the father does not know. The uncertainty casts a vagueness over the scene as a whole, but highlights something else: the outline of the father's consciousness. Our intense experience of the father's consciousness is the result, in this story, of Rulfo's technique of only hinting at things. What is surprising is that the father is prepared to leave things in that degree of uncertainty (instead of attempting to discover the actual state of the son). We realize that this is because he is so wrapped up in his anger — it is the anger which is present to him, more than anything else in the scene. He cannot be physically violent towards his son — that is taboo — but he can try to wring out of him the pity he never showed. At about this point in the story, the son, as we can later surmise, has died. But the father has another, more pressing concern: to exact due pity from him. The son's tears are probably an illusion of the father's, but an illusion which the father converts into a reality: he makes the son express pity, even if that is possible only when the son is dead. The father's determination to exact payment of this debt overrides even the boundary between life and death.

In the last few lines of the story, the father lets the son down onto the ground:

> Destrabó difícilmente los dedos con que su hijo había venido sosteniéndose de su cuello y, al quedar libre, oyó cómo por todas partes ladraban los perros.
> —¿Y tú no los oías, Ignacio? —dijo—. No me ayudaste ni siquiera con esta esperanza. (p.150)

Since there are no lights in the village, the only sign of its proximity would be the barking of dogs. Now we know why the father could not hear: the son's arms, clenched over his head, had covered his ears. So obsessed is he with the son's lack of love that he assumes the son deliberately did not hear. His anger goes beyond death: he speaks to the dead son as if he were alive.

At this point, we have already begun to go back over the story in our minds, to re-read it. The story starts to 'explode', to use Cortázar's word, to reach beyond its limits as anecdote. Now that we know why the father could not, physically, hear, another meaning begins to emerge, where the physical level represents something else. His strange remark to the dead son, 'No me ayudaste ni siquiera con esta esperanza', shows that the son blots out all hope for the father, any vision of the future, any consciousness beyond the rage against the man on his back. So the first haunting image of the two men making a single stumbling shadow in the moonlight returns and takes on new meanings. But why such terrible, extreme hatred, reaching beyond death — like the *tiros de gracia* that disfigure corpses in several of the stories? This is another incitement to make us re-read. There is a clue in the father's feeling that the son killed the mother and in his statement that he is only carrying the son for the mother: involved here is the father's own loss of mother-love which, as we have seen, generates in Rulfo's world a deep violence.

There is a further dimension to this story in the implication that life destroys, rather than preserves and creates. As Angel Rama points out (*15*, p.7), Rulfo reverses the Roman myth of Aeneas carrying his father Anchises from Troy, which symbolizes bringing the past into the future. In the European context, the son replaces the father within a process of continuity. In Latin America, they confront each other violently, testifying to the original and as yet unresolved conflict of civilizations which gave birth to the mestizo culture of countries like Mexico. Violence, as will be seen in the next chapter, is one of the key features of the society in which Rulfo grew up.

2. Mexican History and Society

Rulfo was born in 1918 in the State of Jalisco, to the north-west of Mexico City. He spent his childhood in a part of Jalisco called Los Altos, a highland area which since then has become increasingly barren through deforestation and depopulation. He lost both his parents when he was young: his father died when he was eight years old, his mother a year later. How his father died is something that Rulfo has not revealed, except to the extent of saying that he was killed while fleeing. Violence engulfed the other male members of the family: they all died 'asesinados por la espalda' (*1*, p.30), barring one who met his death in a riding accident. After his mother's death Rulfo was taken to live with his grandmother and at the age of twelve he was sent to an orphanage, an event which must have brought an abrupt end to his childhood and which helps to explain the importance of memory in his work, since from that moment it must have become charged with powerful emotions. The most intensely rendered scenes of childhood are those which involve the memories of Pedro in *Pedro Páramo*; 'Macario' also clearly draws on the first twelve years of Rulfo's life, as do the other stories of the book. Another main motivation of Rulfo's writing is the experience of loneliness: 'el hecho de que escribiera se debía precisamente a eso: parece que quería desahogarme por medio de la soledad en que había vivido, no en la ciudad de México, pero desde hace muchos años, desde que estuve en el orfanatorio' (*1*, p.53).

After the orphanage, he went to Mexico City where he lived with an uncle who made him drop the name Rulfo and use the other family surname, as a result of which he had to call himself Juan Pérez, Rulfo being a name which was frowned upon. He studied law at the University, but failed the examination and took the first of several jobs in the state bureaucracy; since 1962 he has worked in the Instituto Indigenista. By the late 1930s he

had begun to write a novel, *El hijo del desaliento*, which he later
destroyed for being too conventional and long-winded. His first
story to appear in print was 'La vida no es muy seria en sus
cosas', which was not included in *El llano en llamas*; it was
immediately followed, in July 1945, by 'Nos han dado la tierra'.
Other stories followed over the next six years, and the collection
was published in 1953. In 1970 the ninth reimpression (which
should be considered the second edition) was published,
eliminating 'Paso del norte' and including 'El día del derrumbe'
and 'La herencia de Matilde Arcángel', both of which had first
appeared in 1955. The *Obra completa*, published in the
Biblioteca Ayacucho series in 1977, restored 'Paso del norte' to
the collection.

Apart from his other major work, the novel *Pedro Páramo*
which came out in 1955 and which like *El llano en llamas* was
quickly acclaimed as a masterpiece, Rulfo has published nothing
else, except for a few texts for the cinema. This has given him a
reputation as a 'silent' writer, enhanced by the fact that in the
few interviews he has given he is reserved and uncommunicative.
But as Angel Rama has pointed out (*15*, pp.1-2), his silence did
not begin after *Pedro Páramo*: from the beginning his writing
had been bare and unornamented, the result of a great deal of
rewriting and paring down to essentials. Silence had always been
a part of his work.

In *Autobiografía armada*, an assemblage of statements made
by Rulfo in interviews at different times and places, it emerges
that one of the key memories from his early years is the Cristero
war (1926-29). Fought between the government and the
peasantry who lived in areas to the north and west of Mexico
City, principally Michoacán and Jalisco, the war caused the
death of 90,000 combatants and an uncounted number of
civilians. It arose from a conflict between church and state
which had been coming to a head periodically since the nineteenth century. The legitimacy of the modern state requires that
there be no power apart from itself, whereas the church claimed
its own independent sphere of power — a conflict of attitudes
which first emerges historically in the European Middle Ages.
War was triggered by President Calles's prohibition of public

worship. The peasantry immediately saw this as depriving them of a deeply felt right, and took up arms against the Federal (i.e. state) army, in the name of Christ the King: hence the name Cristeros. By 1929 a stalemate had been reached, the Cristeros lacking cash and ammunition and the government unable to impose a military solution: public worship was re-established and peace negotiated. Not all the peasants laid down their arms, and localized skirmishes continued for several years, but the basic issue had been settled, irreversibly, in favour of the state. It has been argued that the Cristeros were a reactionary movement orchestrated by the right, but Meyer shows (*23*, p.213) that the movement was in fact more spontaneous. It would be more accurate to say that the Mexican Revolution had not solved the problems (such as endemic poverty) of the traditional peasantry, and that subsequent reforms (such as Agrarian Reform and the capitalization of agriculture) tended to exacerbate these problems, which are the soil upon which the Cristero revolt was able to grow.

Rulfo speaks in an interview of his memories of the Cristiada:

> La guerra de los cristeros me tocó a mí, parte en mi pueblo y parte en Guadalajara, entre el 26 y el 28. Las primeras guerrillas me tocaron en el pueblo. Tendría yo como 8 años cuando el cura de San Gabriel dejó su biblioteca a guardar en la casa de mi abuela, antes de que expropiaran el curato y lo convirtieran en cuartel. Leí todos los libros que tenía ... Los curas de la costa siempre traen pistola, son curas 'bragados'. El cura Sedano de Zapotlán el Grande (ciudad Guzmán) raptaba muchachas y se aprovechó de la cristiada para alzarse en armas, lo mismo que el de San Gabriel y el de Jiquilpan. A Sedano lo colgaron en un poste del telégrafo. (*1*, pp.38-41)

Los Altos were 'the most solidly Cristero regions' (*23*, p.115); the fact that the local priests took up arms, which was a rarity as Meyer points out, underlines the strength of local involvement in the conflict.

For the rest of this chapter I want to consider Rulfo's view of the peasantry and Mexican history, taking his writing not as providing historical information but as a creative response to history. When Rulfo speaks in interviews about Jalisco and its social conditions, he shows that what interests him is the subjective factor in history; he is concerned with the connection between people's inner consciousness and the way they behave, rather than in sociological explanations of behaviour. The type of issue which concerns him most deeply is why the peasants of Jalisco were so conservative and did not wish to participate in the Agrarian Reform, or why so many of the male members of his family met violent deaths; his fiction is his way of giving an answer. Speaking of *Pedro Páramo*, he traces the inspiration for it back to a visit he made to his childhood town thirty years after leaving. The population had dropped from seven or eight thousand to a hundred and fifty: 'a mí me tocó estar allí una noche, y es un pueblo donde sopla mucho el viento, está al pie de la sierra madre. Y en las noches las casuarinas mugen, aullan ... Cómo aquella gente dejó morir al pueblo. Cómo se justificaba el querer abandonar aquellas cosas. Su casa, todo' (*1*, pp.61-62). The answer to these thoughts is given in the novel, and also in the story 'Luvina'. But there is no attempt at historical comprehensiveness or sociological analysis. As Rulfo says in one of the most precise and comprehensive statements he has made about his art, 'Mi obra no es de periodista ni de etnógrafo, ni de sociólogo. *Lo que hago es una transposición literaria de los hechos de mi conciencia*. La transposición no es una deformación sino el descubrimiento de formas especiales de sensibilidad' (*1*, pp.72-73). He is asking us here to recognize that what may seem to be warped views of reality are in fact special ways of responding — an obvious example of which is Macario's view of the world.

As an overall characterization of how history presses upon the peasantry, Blanco Aguinaga's statement in his important essay on Rulfo is accurate and succinct: for Rulfo's characters, 'la Historia es el enemigo, lo que les ha obligado a encerrarse. Desde la Colonia hasta la actual miseria, la trayectoria es clara' (*4*, p.112). Blanco Aguinaga stresses the characters' withdrawal as a result of the alien force of history, an interpretation which I shall discuss in detail later in this chapter and in Chapter 4. His contention, in general terms, is supported by *Pedro Páramo*, which covers a time-lapse of some three decades, from before the Mexican Revolution to after the Cristero War. The Mexican Revolution, the key event of modern Mexico and one of the major revolutions of the century, bypasses a whole community because the feudal cacique pays off the revolutionaries while the inhabitants identify themselves with the cacique. All news of the Revolution is relayed by a character who stutters, el Tartamudo. The stuttering enacts the distancing of history and its incoherence from the peasants' point of view. In the *Autobiografía* Rulfo characterizes them as 'muy reaccionarios' and as people weighed down by the past: 'Ellos no quieren abandonar a sus muertos. Llevan sus muertos a cuestas' (*1*, pp.34, 38).

The title story 'El llano en llamas' is set in the period of the Mexican Revolution proper, some ten years before the War of the Cristeros. The action is located in Jalisco, and traces the fortunes of a band of peasant revolutionaries, some of whose exploits are indistinguishable from banditry. However, unlike Azuela's *Los de abajo*, the most widely read of all the novels of the Mexican Revolution, Rulfo's story does not place the peasants within a context of moral and social values by which they are judged negatively. We are confronted with a moral blankness which prevents us from judging. The narrator, el Pichón, is a member of the band, but is strangely withdrawn, almost as though everything were happening to someone else. Rodríguez Alcalá points out his moral indifference as he watches the plain, covered with ripe corn, burst into flames (*16*, p.89). But it is not that there is no reference to morality in the story. At the end, Pichón is in jail, not for being a member of Pedro Zamora's band, but 'por otras cosas, entre otras por la mala costumbre que yo tenía de robar muchachas' (p.109). He sees himself as a bad character, but as if this were someone else: the only morality being this conventional, simplistic one to which he bows but which is not really his own — and which he does not live by.

In fact the narrator is as if dazed, like an iguana 'calentándo[se] al sol', as he describes himself and his comrades during a lull in the fighting (p.94). The narrative is one of disconnected events, as is Pichón's perception of the Revolution: there is no rationality to give it shape or direction. The only statement about there being any purpose to it is the rather vague one made by Pedro Zamora, the leader, from which the only certainties to emerge are that it is against the rich and against the government, although 'no tenemos por ahorita ninguna bandera por qué pelear' (p.101). The lack of direction is reflected in the rhythm: they shoot, then get shot at, unaware of where the bullets are coming from. Flocks of birds rise up, startled by the bullets. They disband, come together, then disband again, according to the ebb and flow of the Revolution. And this continues for five years. All helps to create the sensation of history as something alien.

There is a type of childish playfulness to the violence, above all in the 'juego del toro' which Pedro Zamora likes to play: he is the bull, with a rapier for the horns, while the Federal prisoners are the bullfighter, with a blanket for the cape. The bull always wins, if necessary by breaking the rules of the game and using human cunning. Also childish is Pichón's unshocked curiosity about death and destruction: when they find a group of dead comrades, 'les alzamos la cabeza y se la zongoloteamos un poquito para ver si alguno daba todavía señales; pero no, ya estaban bien difuntos. En el aguaje estaba otro de los nuestros con las costillas de fuera como si lo hubieran macheteado' (p.98). His attitude towards the derailing of the train or the burning of the plain is similar. But there is another side to the childishness: an openness and vulnerability which educated people (i.e. those who belong to modern urban culture) do not have. Rulfo has said that for the peasants 'la tristeza debe ser más grande que en las personas cultivadas. Porque esas personas cultivadas tienen corazas para defenderse. Ellos no' (*1*, pp.78-79). They are for this reason capable of expressing an emotional rawness and directness which reaches beneath our own defences, as when Pichón refers to the death of Pedro Zamora, who had been a protective, fatherly figure to the band: 'Es todavía la hora en que no ha vuelto' (p.109).

'La noche que lo dejaron solo' is the story which deals most directly with the Cristero War, although the others are marked by the violent atmosphere of the period. Owing to factors such as the lack of cash and ammunition and the need to continue working the land, the Cristeros used guerrilla tactics rather than forming a standing army. The protagonist and his two companions are a remnant of a guerrilla band, escaping from the Federales to safe territory; they are travelling through the highlands by night, to avoid capture. There is no mention of Cristero ideology, and the protagonist is dazed by sleeplessness: sleep is taking him over, so that he begins to lose his will. When he gives himself to sleep, he risks giving himself to death: his vulnerability, when left behind by the others, is underlined by the title. But actually, and this is one of the deep ironies of the story, it is the other two who die, a fact which underlines the arbitrariness of history. He survives to see them, not resting in the warmth of the sun, as he had imagined them, but hanging from a tree, blackened by the smoke from the soldiers' fire.

The modern urban reader is apt perhaps to forget that the traditional culture of the peasantry was once universal in Western society. As Meyer writes, 'their culture remained rooted in a base which was once common to all and which the elites in the Western world had abandoned at least as early as the eighteenth century' (*23*, p.181). In Mexico the process happened later, the final consolidation of the modern state not occurring until the 1930s and 40s. The Cristero revolt was, among other things, the last attempt of a traditional rural culture to challenge modern political forms of state rule. Rulfo's fiction disallows the modern state, questioning its legitimacy as representative of the population. For instance, in 'Luvina', the protagonist, who is a teacher and therefore a government employee, tells the peasants that the government will help them:

—¿Dices que el Gobierno nos ayudará, profesor? ¿Tú conoces al Gobierno?
Les dije que sí.
—También nosotros lo conocemos. Da esa casualidad. De lo que no sabemos nada es de la madre del Gobierno. (p.127)

The implied saying, 'fulano no tiene madre', which is normally a violent insult, is here not so much an insult as a way of stating that the government exists totally outside the type of parental obligation which was provided in the traditional paternalistic relationship between peasant and feudal landlord. The teacher ends by agreeing with the peasants: the government shows paternal sentiment only when there is a question of punishment: 'El señor ese sólo se acuerda de ellos cuando alguno de sus muchachos ha hecho alguna fechoría acá abajo. Entonces manda por él hasta Luvina y se lo matan. De ahí en más no saben si existe' (p.127). A major reason for the teacher's despair is the fact that his belief in progress has been eaten away by the stubborn reality of the place: the peasants' traditional culture is more powerful than his education. This confrontation points to a feature of Rulfo's work not generally mentioned by critics: its critique of post-Revolutionary *desarrollismo*, i.e. of the notion that the modernisation of the economy and culture in Mexico would create a more genuine national identity.

'El día del derrumbe' traces another confrontation between the peasants' mentality and the alien culture of modern government and bureaucracy. The local governor has come to inspect the damage caused by an earthquake. He is surrounded by a large entourage, which includes a geologist and other 'gente conocedora', all of whom the local people have to feed, putting on a feast which nearly bankrupts them. The centre-piece is the governor's long speech after the meal. He talks on and on, right through a drunken gunfight which breaks out among the guests. This part is recounted by a peasant who remembers word-for-word the pompous, empty, bureaucratic language. It is a meeting of two worlds, separated by language, by culture, and by relationship to history. Rulfo's treatment of these themes is humorous (this, with 'Anacleto Morones', is the most humorous of the stories), and the humour helps to communicate the peasants' perceptions. The government party appropriate to themselves the right to speak for Mexican history. This does not impress the peasants:

Habló de Juárez que nosotros teníamos levantado en la plaza y hasta entonces supimos que era la estatua de Juárez, pues nunca nadie nos había podido decir quién era el individuo que estaba encaramado en el monumento aquel. (p.153)

Rulfo draws on the rural culture of Jalisco in order to confront the modern urban reader with realities that do not fit into his world because they have been suppressed in one way or another. This culture is an oral one, a fact to which Rulfo has responded by giving his fiction a predominantly oral character (see Chapter 7, below). This coincides with Meyer's view of the position that the historian needs to adopt *vis à vis* the Cristero rebellion: 'he must be mindful of the fact that he is involved with a popular culture whose lively traditions derived from the Middle Ages and the sixteenth century' (*23*, p.181). In the story 'Nos han dado la tierra' the oral emphasis begins with the title, which indicates what the characters say about their situation, this not being the same, necessarily, as what they really think about it. It is what they are supposed to say, the language expected by the authorities, or by history, but uttered ironically.

The land referred to is the land they have been given by the Agrarian Reform, land redistribution being one of the original goals of the Revolution but in the post-Revolutionary period one of the main methods to extend government control over the rural areas. Agrarian Reform began in a minor way in the 1920s, with major redistributions in the 1930s, which is the period that the story, first published in 1945, probably refers to. The peasants in the story have been offered the barren worthless land of the high plain, as a result of the collusion, implied though not spelt out, between the government and the local landowners. A newspaper report from 1964, quoted by Donald K. Gordon, shows that this practice has a continuing history in Mexico. 'RECHAZAN LOS CAMPESINOS LAS TIERRAS ESTÉRILES EN LA LAGUNA Y P. NEGRAS ... De los 227 campesinos que serían "Beneficiados", sólo uno se presentó a la hora del reparto. Indícase que las haciendas, obligadas a ceder parte de sus tierras, escogieron las peores, solapadas por el gobierno local' (*7*, p.63).

The rhythm of the story is that of the movement of the peasants, slow after many hours of walking. Their thinking also takes on a similar rhythm, slowed-down and deliberate. The story is not so much about its plot, which by all accounts is very simple, as about a slow process of recognition on the part of the reader that the peasants have been sold down the river: the more they block it out, the more the reader realizes it. The response of the government official to their complaints is at first one of condescending cynicism; then, when they insist, the official hides behind a mask of government ideology: '—Eso manifiéstenlo por escrito. Y ahora váyanse. Es al latifundio al que tienen que atacar, no al Gobierno que les da la tierra' (p.42). These are the official's final words. He will not listen any more: writing serves him as a weapon to defend himself and what he represents, while for the peasants this instrument of the enemy culture cuts off all further interchange. As the narrator stresses, 'no nos dejaron decir nuestras cosas' (p.41).

The peasants' response is not at first easy to understand. They seem perhaps strangely submissive, given that the land is utterly useless: 'Espérenos usted, señor delegado. Nosotros no hemos dicho nada contra el Centro. Todo es contra el Llano ... No se puede contra lo que no se puede. Eso es lo que hemos dicho ...' (p.42). Is this a case of fatalism? But fatalism is a cliché of Rulfo criticism, which is used as a catch-all explanation. It needs to be examined carefully, as a preliminary discussion here will show. In taking the *llano* as the enemy and not the government, the peasants are mistaking political conditions for a product of nature. Given that the disguising of politics as nature, i.e. as what cannot be questioned or disputed, is a classic feature of political oppression in its attempts to legitimate itself, are the peasants failing to acknowledge the real enemy, who is hidden behind a screen of fatalism? A clue is given in Frantz Fanon's discussion of resistance to oppression in *The Wretched of the Earth*: when the native is not able to unleash his anger against the settler, 'the native manages to bypass the settler. A belief in fatality removes all blame from the oppressor' (*19*, p.42). Fanon is writing about a colonial situation, but there is a similarity with

Rulfo's Mexico since in both cases the oppressor belongs to a different culture, and so the particular dynamics of oppression are comparable.

Does the peasants' sense of having to accept derive from socio-economic causes, or from existential ones? Rulfo makes us ask the question, but rather than giving a direct answer, provides sufficient information from which to work one out. The peasants' anger is deprived of an outlet by the authorities who hide behind their bureaucratic mask; if their anger cannot be turned against its real cause, then a substitute must be found. Instead of turning it against themselves, which as Fanon shows is the most negative response to this type of situation, they turn it in the direction of nature — a move in harmony with the predominant role allotted to nature in traditional pre-capitalist cultures, where work is dominated by the agricultural cycle and the events of a person's life interpreted against a backdrop of events in nature.

The conversation with the government delegate is a flashback: it occurred before the slow walk over the *llano* described in the first two and a half pages of the story. Unlike the reader, the peasants knew all the time that they had been cheated. Why then go at all to the land they had been given? The answer lies in the shifting of their anger onto the land, through which they achieve a type of self-composure, just as Fanon describes how the native 'by a kind of interior restabilization acquires a stony calm' (*19*, p.42). The journey over the plain is a way of coming to terms with what had happened to them, with the violence of their existence. In fact what happens to them on the plain is symmetrical with what occurred previously in their encounter with the government delegate. Just as they were prevented from speaking to him, so the suffocating plain takes away their words:

No decimos lo que pensamos. Hace ya tiempo que se nos acabaron las ganas de hablar. Se nos acabaron con el calor ... Uno platica aquí y las palabras se calientan en la boca con el calor de afuera, y se le resecan a uno en la lengua, hasta que acaban con el resuello. Aquí así son las cosas.

(p.40)

Their attitude becomes, as they walk on, a type of indifference. The reader's process of recognition that they have been cheated is matched by an opposite movement on their part, the achievement of indifference. The interaction of these two processes reveals the great artistry of the story and accounts for its deep impact.

The peasants' indifference is brought home at the end of the story when they come down from the plain to the rich green lands of the village and the narrator remarks, with a type of resignation, 'la tierra que nos han dado está allá arriba' (p.44). This attitude is not the same as submission, which would imply some degree of identification with the oppressor, nor is it mere apathy, which would imply a complete lack of emotional response. Like other works of the 1940s and 50s, such as Camus's *L'Etranger* (*The Outsider*) or Pinter's *The Caretaker*, Rulfo's stories explore types of consciousness which are outside the dominant ideology or morality but which do not oppose it in a directly political way. By remaining indifferent, Rulfo's peasants avoid giving recognition to the enemy culture through either submission or aggression. They are able to keep an identity for themselves, instead of being drawn into the sphere of official ideology, which would remove them from their traditions and turn them into mere ciphers.

3. *Violence*

There is violence in all of Rulfo's stories, and in several of them it is the dominant theme. Two aspects which stand out are its frequency and the casual way in which it occurs. Referring to the violence of the area in which he grew up, Rulfo says 'importa muy poco la vida'; and, 'no les importa que los maten en cualquier momento' (*1*, pp.31, 32). In order to understand the attitudes to murder, the most frequent form of violence in the stories, we have to realize that violence is not a personal issue in Rulfo's world: if existence itself is violent you do not choose personally whether to be violent or not — in fact there is a sense in which the murderer and the victim stand for the whole community. Because there is an underlying, primary violence (see above, p.12), when overt violence occurs in an act of murder, it does not cause surprise. The stories are not concerned with a moral response to violence. And although from the information Rulfo gives us we can surmise the main social causes (poverty, social injustice, prevalence of banditry), this is not the aspect in which he is most interested. Violence is met with indifference, in that it does not produce anxiety, but there is also a special emotional intensity around it, almost an ecstatic state. The stories express a poetry of violence. Through violence, the characters gain access to an instinctive-irrational level of being, which resists reduction to ethical, sociological or legal explanation. For the perpetrator, violence does not arise consciously; for the victim, it penetrates the body without warning, often in sleep: all deaths but one are the result of the penetration of the body by bullets, knives and other objects. The exception is Tanilo's in 'Talpa', where the whole body erupts outwards.

Let us begin to consider some of these issues as they arise in the story 'El hombre'. This is the most complicated of Rulfo's stories, and therefore it will be useful to begin by showing how the plot works as the reader puts together the various fragments.

The subject is a pursuit: José Alcancía is being pursued by the man whose son he has killed. The feud, however, started further back. Alcancía's brother was killed by this man. Alcancía went to take revenge, but since he arrived at the house at night when the family were asleep, he could not distinguish one person from another and killed all of them, apart from the man he meant to kill, who was away at a funeral. What he does not know is that he is being pursued by the man he thinks he has killed. The narrative alternates between the viewpoint of Alcancía and of the man who is pursuing him, and switches in time from after the murder of the family to before it and vice versa.

At the second reading this fragmented narrative attains a dramatic coherence. At each point we have to decide which of the two men's viewpoints we are being presented with, something which we can do only by entering into the mind of each man and gauging his thoughts and perceptions. When Alcancía murdered the family with a machete, he cut off one of his own toes: 'Cuando sentí que me había cortado un dedo, la gente lo vio y yo no, hasta después. Así ahora, aunque no quiera, tengo que tener alguna señal' (p.63). This grotesque detail adds dramatic force to the beginning, where the pursuer scrutinizes Alcancía's tracks: 'Pies planos —dijo el que le seguía—. Y un dedo de menos. Le falta el dedo gordo en el pie izquierdo. No abundan fulanos con estas señas. Así que será fácil' (p.60). The reader's thinking and Alcancía's work in opposite directions. While the reader puts the details together to make them cohere, and thus become meaningful, Alcancía's awareness is delayed, partial and fragmented, keeping at bay the awful coherence of what he has done. The way the two attitudes engage and contrast with each other generates a major proportion of this story's power to involve the reader.

As the story develops, the alternating viewpoints produce a kind of dialogue between the two men, a form of hidden communication in which the crossing of distance and time heightens the dramatic effect. The core of the story is the violent murder of the family. This must recur (in the sense of being recalled or retold) more often than any other single act in Rulfo's work. Alcancía himself returns to it five times, and his pursuer twice.

What is the point of giving this multiple, refracted image of the act instead of a direct immediate view of it? The answer is that a direct image would fall flat; it would be impossible to capture the full weight and horror of the act. The multiple murder is too unutterable to be faced frontally. And so we get a series of details: that Alcancía crossed himself three times, that the machete got blunt, that with the groans of the first victim he was afraid that the others were going to wake up and he said, 'Discúlpenme la apuración', and so on. The intermittent details are more charged with intensity than would be a full, coherent image.

Alcancía is killed at the end. Instead of narrating this through the pursuer, Rulfo introduces a third character: a shepherd who has witnessed the last days of Alcancía's life and is answering questions put to him by a magistrate. He does not see Alcancía's murder, only its results:

> Primero creí que se había doblado al empinarse sobre el río
> y no había podido ya enderezar la cabeza y que luego se
> había puesto a resollar agua, hasta que le vi la sangre
> coagulada que le salía por la boca y la nuca repleta de
> agujeros como si lo hubieran taladrado. (p.69)

Rulfo uses the shepherd's oblique view not simply to add interest but to make the final act sudden and unforeseen, though expected. For in Rulfo we always see violence afterwards. We never see it coming.

The beginning, as with the beginning of 'No oyes ladrar los perros', suggests a primitive level of reality. The murderer is simply called 'el hombre', as in the title, drawing attention to his basic existence as a human being. But it is not precisely as a human being that the first paragraph presents him to us:

> Los pies del hombre se hundieron en la arena, dejando una
> huella sin forma, como si fuera la pezuña de algún animal.
> Treparon sobre las piedras, engarruñándose al sentir la
> inclinación de la subida, luego caminaron hacia arriba,
> buscando el horizonte. (p.60)

The feet seem to act independently of the man's will and intention, as if his body had taken him over. Then, taking us even further from individual human identity, the man becomes like an animal, both in the direct comparison ('como si fuera ...') and in the word 'engarruñándose', derived from *garra*. His animality is to be understood not in a moral sense, but as embodying an instinctive-irrational level, where morality does not enter. This level becomes overlaid as the story proceeds, and the man and his pursuer become more individualized and their violence accounted for in terms of particular motivation; nevertheless it remains in the background of our awareness, surfacing from time to time, particularly in the ending.

There is a particular stillness and intensity to the final image, Alcancía's corpse as seen by the shepherd: 'la nuca repleta de agujeros como si lo hubieran taladrado' (p.69). The violence inscribed in the still features of the inert corpse exemplifies the special aura which surrounds violence in the story. It is as if time had slowed down to a standstill and the normal flow of life had been arrested, as the image draws everything into itself. This timelessness connects with the inevitability of revenge, violence breeding violence: 'Mañana estarás muerto', says the pursuer, 'o tal vez pasado mañana o dentro de ocho días. No importa el tiempo' (p.65). Georges Bataille's discussion of violence in *El erotismo* helps to explain the aura produced by violence. For Bataille, culture places boundaries (interdicts, or prohibitions) around life in order to protect human beings from the basic violence of sexuality and death. Paradoxically, transgression of the interdict gives access to the sacred. Bataille argues that it is difficult to understand this because Christianity denies the sacredness of transgression, since it responds to the breaking of the law merely with moral condemnation. Before Christianity or outside it violence can be 'una voluntad de acceder al secreto del ser' (*18*, pp.95, 126-27). Thus in Rulfo's world, which is not fundamentally a Christian one, although violence arises out of a loss of social control, it is not merely anarchy or chaos; it gives access to a different order of being, in which human beings are bound together by other, less rational, ties.

There is an impersonal aspect to the killing, as is brought out in the details of Alcancía's perceptions. For instance, in order to explain to himself how it was that he came to kill the whole family, he recalls 'estaba oscuro y los bultos eran iguales', where their bodies are perceived as mere 'bultos' (p.63). There is also a childlike quality in the way Alcancía, in the middle of hacking up the family with his machete, said 'Discúlpeme la apuración' (p.65). To an extent, he is unaware of what he is doing (if one uses the present tense, this is the tense in which the reader makes sense of the murder). For instance, when he cuts off his big toe, 'la gente lo vio y yo no, hasta después' (p.63): we conclude that the intensity of the experience is so great that it somehow anaesthetizes him, blotting out everything else. There is an atmosphere almost of ritual to it, produced by the slowed-down time and altered consciousness.

In this, the most violent of Rulfo's stories, violence reveals its paradoxical features. As we have seen, the alternating viewpoints of the two men become a dialogue. In this way, violence becomes itself a form of communication. Moreover, there is a close relationship between violence and tenderness, each generating an awareness of the other, as is brought home in a series of details which show the terrible vulnerability of the human body. For instance, the victims are murdered in their sleep, a state of total defencelessness. We are told of the difficulties caused by the toughness of human skin and the bluntness of the machete, and later of the nest which Alcancía's body made for itself in the thickets. The physicality of the pursuer is also emphasized: 'Tengo mi corazón que resbala y da vueltas en su propia sangre' (p.65). When Alcancía is close to death, we see the violence of life taking possession of him as much as it did of his victims. This concords with Bataille's view of killing as participation in an inherent violence which already exists rather than as a single separate act: 'Se echó de vuelta al río y la corriente se soltó zangoloteándolo como un reguilete, y hasta por poco se ahoga. Dio muchos manotazos y por fin no pudo pasar y salió allá abajo, echando buches de agua hasta desentriparse' (p.66). The image is of a body thrown about and torn apart, which prepares us for the final image of the bullet holes in the neck, a body totally penetrated by violence.

At one moment the violence of the action is interrupted by the lyrical image of a river:

> Muy abajo el río corre mullendo sus aguas entre sabinos florecidos; meciendo su espesa corriente en silencio. Camina y da vueltas sobre sí mismo. Va y viene como una serpentina enroscada sobre la tierra verde. No hace ruido.
>
> (p.62)

The landscape does not mirror the mood of the characters, it acts as a contrast, providing a silent backdrop to the harsh staccato of the killings. The soft flow of the river, which suggests the flow of time, contrasts with the consciousness of the men, wrapped in timeless imperatives of revenge. This is one of those important though infrequent occasions in the book when a vision of nature as tender and fertile suggests an alternative to a world suffused by violence.

Another story constructed around a core of violence is 'La cuesta de las comadres'. Set in a depopulated zone, it begins by tracing the social reasons for local hatred of the Torrico family. The first part is about the history of the Cuesta and the narrator's discovery that the Torricos are thieves and murderers, a fact at which he shows no surprise. On the contrary, he stresses several times that he was their friend. What does concern him is that he has become too old for violent physical exertion. These two details prepare us for the surprise of the second part. This begins with the statement that he killed Remigio Torrico, which is repeated at the beginning of the next two paragraphs. When Remigio arrives on the scene, all attention is on 'de qué tamaño era su coraje' (p.51), this word being used in its Mexican meaning of anger. There is a slow build-up. The dangerousness of the situation is signalled by the fact that Remigio blames him for the death of his brother and leaves him no space to reply (the narrator in fact knows who the killer was). And yet despite this, and despite the narrator's insistence that it was he who killed Remigio, when it comes to describing the action, he seems almost absent-minded: 'Pero al quitarse él de enfrente, la luz de la luna hizo brillar la aguja de arria, que yo había clavado en el costal. Y no sé por qué, pero de pronto comencé a tener una fe muy grande en aquella aguja' (p.52). The focus is on the needle, not on his feelings or intentions. Expressions like 'pero', 'no sé' and 'de pronto' indicate that there was no foreseeing on his part, and that the act of killing caught him unawares.

The scene takes place in the shadowy light of the moon: the needle glints, emerging from the surrounding darkness. The abruptness of the switch from friendship to violence suggests that the latter, as it emerges from the shadows, is in some way more fundamental. As he looks back to the time when it occurred, the narrator continually announces the murder — or rather, seems to, since it is only by dint of his retrospective view that the murder can be announced to the reader before it occurs. But the fact that the reader's expectancy is aroused gives a greater impact to the narrator's blankness. He did not foresee his action; it was not in his mind. On the other hand, when it occurs, he shows no surprise. This is the nature of violence in Rulfo's world: it is seen as normal, after the event, but at the time it comes from an unknown direction, outside awareness.

The terrible details of Remigio's death create an aura of intensified meaning. This violent core sends its energies radiating through the rest of the story. Each detail is a further tightening of the rack of agony as violence invades the man's body. While he dies there is what at first sight might appear to be a perverse tenderness in the way the old man describes him: 'vi que se le iba entristeciendo la mirada como si comenzara a sentirse enfermo. Hacía mucho que no me tocaba ver una mirada así de triste y me entró la lástima. Por eso aproveché para sacarle la aguja de arria del ombligo y metérsela más arribita, allí donde pensé que tendría el corazón. Y sí, allí lo tenía, porque nomás dio dos o tres respingos como un pollo descabezado y luego se quedó quieto' (p.53). But the note of tenderness is not really a sign of perversity. The old man is sensitive to Remigio's agony — albeit in a way which may seem childlike or amoral to us. It is almost as if he identified himself with Remigio: to kill is to participate in the basic violence which is the unconscious and physical ground of existence, in the violence of life which in Rulfo's world binds people together, in a kind of

communion. Octavio Paz, in his discussion of the role of death
in Mexican culture, writes of the relationship which killing
establishes between murderer and victim: 'Para nosotros el
crimen es todavía una relación ... De ahí su dramatismo, su
poesía' (*24*, p.55).

It may be helpful, in conclusion to this chapter, to consider
briefly episodes of violence in other stories. Some of these will
be discussed again later on, in connection with other issues; the
purpose here is to substantiate the assertion that killings bring
about a trance-like state. In 'Díles que no me maten' we are told
twice that the protagonist, Juvencio Nava, had to kill don Lupe
('tuvo que matar a don Lupe'), the thought being that given a
certain situation he had no choice, something else took over his
personal will. In 'En la madrugada' the cowherd Esteban kills
don Justo in a fight, but does not remember how he did it: his
consciousness has been blotted out. The main episode of 'Talpa'
is the death of Tanilo, a death willed by his brother and by
Natalia. The death is a long, slow process ending with a frenzied
dance which recalls the medieval Dance of Death and which
illustrates the connection between death and ritual in Rulfo's
world. The ritual meaning of death in traditional Mexican
culture is compared by Octavio Paz with the ritual breaking of
social norms in the Fiesta: 'la Fiesta ... es una revuelta, una
súbita inmersión en lo informe, en la vida pura. A través de la
Fiesta la sociedad se libera de las normas que se ha impuesto'
(*24*, p.46).

4. Law, Guilt and Indifference

The trance-like states referred to in the previous chapter and the blotting out of awareness occurring, for instance, in 'Macario' and 'No oyes ladrar los perros' are among the most disturbing features of Rulfo's stories. The most significant attempt to explain these phenomena has been that of Blanco Aguinaga. In a key formulation of his point of view, he states: 'En esta tensión angustiosa entre la lentitud interior y la violencia externa está el secreto de la visión de la realidad mexicana en Rulfo. Esa realidad fatalista, estática, de hombres y mujeres solos, hacia adentro' (4, p.97). It should be stressed that Blanco Aguinaga assumes that fatalism is produced in the characters by the impact of the violence of the world they live in, i.e. that their internal state can be accounted for by an external reality. The same assumption is made in his description of the characters of *Pedro Páramo*: 'el mismo fatalismo frente al mecánico y brutal acontecer exterior' (4, p.98). A further assumption emerges when at the end of his essay he summarizes the relationship between Rulfo's characters and history: 'estos hombres y mujeres se ven reducidos a vivir por dentro, sin tiempo, es decir, al margen de la Historia o bajo ella' (4, p.112). Here the word *reducidos* is used to point to the process which has brought about the fatalism, a process which assumes the characters to be passive. What is questionable about this argument is the presupposition that the external world is presented in the stories as independent of the characters' state of mind, and ultimately accountable for their state of mind.

This is not to say that the external world which Blanco Aguinaga characterizes as brutal and mechanical cannot be clearly recognized in nearly all the stories. Its features are monotony, lack of colour, and the emotional flatness of the description: it has the characteristics of a desert, both literally and metaphorically. But internal and external reality cannot be separated:

what is internal is experienced as external, and vice versa. For instance, on the one hand, the desert landscapes reveal, at the level of perception, the inward emotional withdrawal of the characters; or else, it is only in the external aspects of murder (weapons, corpse, moonlight, etc.) that the inward impulse to kill figures. On the other hand, a particular landscape becomes an inward emotional state, above all in 'Luvina'. Both types of process can occur simultaneously, as with the river in 'Es que somos muy pobres', which the boy narrator sees as both inside his sister and external to her, converting it into a notion of fate which overrides any distinction between internal and external worlds. Thus the boundary between inward (= subjective) and outward (= objective), normal in our own culture and typical of the traditional realist novel, tends to be erased. *Pedro Páramo* takes this principle a step further, by allowing fantasy and hallucination into the narrated world and treating it as an objective reality. In this sense, Rulfo is, with Alejo Carpentier, a pioneer of what has been called magical realism, as is borne out by García Márquez's statement that he could not have written *Cien años de soledad* had he not read *Pedro Páramo*.

At one point, referring to 'Talpa', Blanco Aguinaga recognizes that it is not merely that the external world affects the internal but that the reverse can also occur: 'todo el acontecer del mundo de los hechos, exterior, parece haberse achatado en el meditar obstinado desde dentro' (*4*, p.96). The flattening process is a result of emotional withdrawal. But it is dynamic, not passive or merely apathetic. It produces the indifference through which the characters confront their environment and which in 'Nos han dado la tierra' is adopted as a way of confronting social oppression without releasing all the accumulated hatred in open rebellion, an action which would lead to the defeat of the peasants. The concept of indifference corrects the lack of dynamic features in Blanco Aguinaga's passive model of the inner world of the characters. It should also be noted that indifference is not the same as denial, which, while wishing to get rid of what is denied, at the same time confirms it. Nor does it include an assertion of alternative values: it is not in fact concerned with values. What it does is to refuse recognition to what it confronts, like the attitude which Octavio Paz describes as 'ningunear' (*24*, p.40).

It is thus inappropriate to apply the concept of a separate inner world to Rulfo's characters. This may seem to be contradicted by the fact, stressed particularly by Joseph Sommers, that Rulfo is not a social realist but a writer concerned with subjective realities (*27*, pp.75-76). But the key word here is separate: Rulfo's stories break down the boundary between inward and outward, subjective and objective. Characters do not identify the impulse to kill as inward, nor the act of killing as outward either, in the sense of there being a tellable objective version of it. The separation we should tend to make does not work. Thus Blanco Aguinaga's approach restores the private individualism which the text breaks down. Rulfo's characters do not live according to a comfortable separation between inner and outer: they are continually invaded by the violence of the external world, which in turn reflects the violence they carry within them. Because they have no faith in a separate, outer, objective reality, there is no sharply delineated inner world for them either. As an extension of this, the notion of truth in Rulfo's world does not rest on individual conscience. There are cases where characters do not remember whether they have killed, while allowing that this might have happened ('Macario', 'En la madrugada'). This does not mean that there is no truth at all, but that the usual criteria for objective truth are missing: objective truth belongs to the social and legal systems, towards which the characters are indifferent. In 'Nos han dado la tierra', for instance, the peasants cannot speak their truth to the government representative. Of course the reader is not limited to the position of the characters, since we have at our disposal what the story says about itself, which includes historical, social and psychological information, as well as the reader's ability to grasp the story as a whole, instead of being confined to any one character's viewpoint. Nevertheless, no objective truth is provided by authorial guarantee for us to rely upon, and we are brought back to the particular qualities of the characters' consciousness as the basis of our relationship with the story and its world.

The fact that the characters lack certain cultural elements that we have (such as individual conscience) does not mean that their world is a simplified one or that it does not speak to our condition. Their lack of individual conscience subverts the liberal notion of private conscience as the definition of a person's relationship with truth and with society. Lacking a modern sense of participation in society as individuals, they do not have a compensating sense of belonging to a traditional community. There are vestiges of traditional belief, such as attitudes to the dead, echoes of myths, but they are only vestiges, not parts of a functioning cultural system. The characters are dislocated: they do not belong fully either to a traditional society or to the modern world.

The story which best exemplifies the disturbing lack of conscience is 'En la madrugada'. What surprises the reader most is the old cowherd Esteban's uncertainty as to whether he killed his boss or not: 'que dizque yo lo había matado, dijeron los díceres. Bien pudo ser, pero yo no me acuerdo' (p.73). That he did not remember the details would be easy to accept, since at a certain point he must have lost consciousness. But to say that he does not remember whether he killed or not — this is hard for us to accept, since we would expect him to make up his mind one way or the other as to whether he was responsible for don Justo's death. The idea that he killed don Justo is something external to him, on the level of rumours (*díceres*) put about by other people. He is speaking to an unnamed person in jail (a cell-mate, possibly), and his words show that it is irrelevant to him whether he is responsible or not: 'Pero desde el momento que me tienen aquí en la cárcel por algo ha de ser, ¿no cree usted?' (p.73). Our own cultural attitudes would make such ambiguity intolerable, since one would need to know how far one is responsible, however unjust the legal system. Esteban neither accepts nor rejects the legal system; acknowledging that it has power over him, he remains indifferent to it. Bourgeois legality and its inward inscription in conscience is contested, the story testifying to other, more archaic, rules, related to abused or lost mothers and tabooed desires.

Esteban does not think in terms of being guilty or innocent of murder because he is not conscious of an internal impulse to kill don Justo. To work out how this can be so we need to consider the story as a whole. If we reconstruct the events, they are as follows: Esteban arrives back at the farm at dawn with the herd of cows; as the *patrón* is not there, he jumps over the fence and lets himself in. At that moment he sees don Justo carrying his own niece, with whom he has spent the night, across the corral, and he hides. One of the cows has to be separated from its calf. Esteban is angry with the calf for being greedy for the milk and begins to kick its head. Don Justo discovers him, and a fight ensues in which don Justo is killed. Esteban wakes up after a period of unconsciousness, goes home, and is arrested for murder. This was the sequence of events, but they are not told either directly or in this order. The structure of time is crucially important: the events are mainly recalled by Esteban in jail, possibly a considerable time after they occurred (the amount of time that has elapsed is left vague). They are events which have already occurred, and the feeling is that nothing can be done about them. Another important feature is the atmosphere. The imagery of the opening paragraphs is of night, sleep, tenderness and vulnerability: 'Las nubes de la noche durmieron sobre el pueblo buscando el calor de la gente. Ahora está por salir el sol y la niebla se levanta despacio, enrollando su sábana, dejando hebras blancas encima de los tejados' (p.70). As the sun rises and day comes, the atmosphere of warmth and protection is shattered by violence.

The details of the violence are unemphatic (the flatness derives from how they are seen by Esteban) and we have to read them as signs of his mind — without, however, psychologizing him, because this would amount to providing him with a set of private motivations and thus putting onto him the kind of individuality and social rationality which the story does not give him. The signs are outward and inward, both at once. For instance, the crucial detail of Esteban's kicking the calf, although an apparently unjustifiable and inexplicable action, can be interpreted if we place it beside a set of other details which are given. The calf is taking its mother's milk at a time when this should be prohibited since the cow is about to calve. Don Justo, whom

Esteban has just seen crossing the yard, is also doing something forbidden: committing incest with his niece. A passing detail now reveals its significance: Esteban, when he saw Don Justo with his niece in his arms, hid himself, showing his recognition that what he has seen is tabooed. The calf and the *patrón* both represent taking what is forbidden, and this in both cases has to do with love. The atmosphere of tenderness in the first paragraph, where the sheets of mist suggest the soft bed and, by extension, the emotional warmth which Esteban lacks, points to his emotional deprivation. If we bear in mind the detail of mother's milk, then Esteban becomes comparable with Macario; the calf he kicks is taking (metaphorically) what he wants, and so also is don Justo. Kicking the calf is also a way of getting back at his boss, the emotional dimension coinciding with that of social oppression: 'Todo le parecía mal: hasta que yo estuviera flaco no le gustaba. Y cómo no iba a estar flaco si apenas comía' (p.75). At the end a detail is added which paradoxically confirms don Justo's oppressive role: on the night of his funeral the town is in darkness, 'pues don Justo era el dueño de la luz' (p.75).

Esteban's attitude to don Justo's death as something occurring outside the sphere of his awareness is further brought home by the way he narrates the fact of the death: '¿Qué pasó luego? Yo no lo supe. No volví a trabajar con él. Ni yo ni nadie, porque ese mismo día se murió' (p.72). The fight itself is surrounded with darkness. The only account we have of it is a brief description of don Justo's sensations, in the fifth section which is recounted from the latter's point of view. At the end of the section he loses consciousness, and beyond this we know nothing. The lack of information is not a blank which we are left to fill in at our own whim. Rulfo's concern is not to present an objective scene, but to dramatize a consciousness. Esteban's consciousness is illuminated for us as much by what he does not know as by what he does. Thus, as Rodríguez Alcalá notes (*16*, p.21), it is irrelevant to conjecture that a third person might have come on the scene and caused the death of don Justo. On the other hand, when Rodríguez Alcalá tries to explain Esteban by speaking about impenetrability and *hermetismo* he is misleading

(*16*, pp.21-23): Esteban's mind is in fact quite open to the reader who becomes attuned to it. But the way it works, contrary to normal thinking, is disturbing. Esteban accepts the uncertainty, without reaching after fact and reason in order to resolve it. Obviously, at some point in the fight he must have become unconscious, but we do not know when, and what is notable is that he does not try to reconstruct what happened, by deduction. He is able to leave the uncertainty unresolved. For the reader, the story raises the issue of how little we really know of ourselves or others and how far we invent certainties.

What Rulfo conveys to us of the legal system (which is a function of the State) is that justice cannot be expected from it. It is concerned only with producing criminals. For instance, in the final part of 'El hombre' the magistrate is trying to frame the witness, a classic manoeuvre of a system which needs to produce convictions and which assumes guilt unless innocence can be proven. In this world, once you are in the hands of the law you are guilty. Rulfo's characters are indifferent towards this type of law, and give a different meaning to the word *ley*. Speaking about how the men abandon the village to the women and old people, the protagonist of 'Luvina' says, 'Es la costumbre. Allí le dicen la ley, pero es lo mismo' (p.126). As Blanco Aguinaga points out, this is to conflate nature (the biological law of life and death) with the socio-political level (*4*, p.113). What we are witnessing here is probably the vestige of a traditional system of social regulation, based on the rhythm of natural events. The peasants refuse the official legal system as a regulation of their lives and at the same time place themselves under the sway of a law of life which removes moral choice and responsibility. This helps us to understand how it is, as Harss has very accurately asserted (*8*, p.320), that all the characters are guilty, but none responsible. There is a type of primary guilt, which cannot be altered by what any of them do. It is nowhere better expressed than in a remark by Susana San Juan, in *Pedro Páramo*: '¿Y qué crees que es la vida, Justina, sino un pecado?' (*3*, p.113). The pressure of this more fundamental guilt pushes legal guilt into second place. Bourgeois legality is kept at a distance so as to reveal the conflict of desire and taboo which takes place beneath the characters' external indifference.

In 'Talpa' there is no guilt in a legal sense, but on a deeper
level, because they wanted Tanilo to die, the narrator and
Natalia are guilty in relation to fundamental taboos against the
murder of a brother and a husband. The structure is such that,
as in so many of the stories, a narrator goes back over past
events whose meaning at the time was not clear. The reader is
involved together with the narrator in the process of discovering
meaning, of recognition of what really happened: thus the story
does not start with a set of events to be elaborated, rather the
events become part of a story only insofar as the question of
their meaning is being raised. A summary of the events would be
roughly as follows: the narrator and his brother's wife, who
desire each other, take the sick brother on a pilgrimage to Talpa
in the hope that he will die. But the present with which the story
starts and from which it is told is the return from Talpa, when
Natalia threw herself into her mother's arms and cried and
would have nothing to do with the narrator. During the
pilgrimage they had not been aware they wanted to kill Tanilo; it
is only afterwards that they are able to recognize the wish. Thus
a reconstructed account of the events is bound to falsify the
story. The wish to kill and the awareness of it are mutually
exclusive, and separated by a gulf in time.

During the pilgrimage Natalia's and her brother-in-law's
awareness is dominated by the feeling that the horribly decaying
body of Tanilo comes between them: 'sentíamos que sus manos
ampolladas se metían entre nosotros' (p.78). But as soon as he
dies, the pity they had not felt before takes possession of them:

> Afuera se oía el ruido de las danzas; los tambores y la
> chirimía; el repique de las campanas. Y entonces fue
> cuando me dio a mí tristeza. Ver tantas cosas vivas: ver a la
> Virgen allí, mero enfrente de nosotros dándonos su
> sonrisa, y ver por el otro lado a Tanilo, como si fuera un
> estorbo. Me dio tristeza. (pp.84-85)

The pathetic aspect of the plot is brought home: Tanilo went to
the miraculous shrine of Talpa hoping that his life would be

saved; the other two in the hope that he would die. And the pity triggers and feeds their guilt, which in turn makes Tanilo more alive once they have killed him: his corpse begins to haunt them, and on the return journey they are unable to touch each other. Thus it emerges that the problem was not Tanilo's physical presence, but their guilt, which it represented, which it literally embodied. But this knowledge is now useless, separated by a gulf of time from the moment when it could have prevented them from trying to solve things through Tanilo's death.

The opposition between desire on the one hand and pity and guilt on the other is echoed by the contrast between two types of reality, the animal and the human, the former threatening to engulf and destroy the latter. As pointed out in Chapter 2, the power of the animal level of existence is that it brings about a suspension of morality; in 'Talpa' a further consequence emerges: the possibility that the human might be destroyed by the animal. During the pilgrimage the people become like 'gusanos apelotonados bajo el sol', and the noise of their prayers is like the lowing of cattle (pp.81, 82). There is particular weight in this comparison, since prayer is of course meant to raise human beings to a higher level. In the church in Talpa, their prayers are again compared to the noise of animals: 'un ruido igual al de muchas avispas espantadas por el humo' (p.84). The specific mark of humanity, the ability to communicate through language, becomes a merely animal noise. But Tanilo's decaying body is the main place where the human becomes animal. The pus from his wounds is like 'goma de copal' (p.77) and he exudes a smell like a dead animal which penetrates everywhere: his skin, the usual boundary of the self, no longer contains him. There is something deeply inhuman about the ghastly degeneration of his body. And there is no relief from the horror until the last words of the story, when Tanilo is buried:

Es de eso de lo que quizá no acordemos aquí más seguido: de aquel Tanilo que nosotros enterramos en el camposanto de Talpa; al que Natalia y yo echamos tierra y piedras encima para que no lo fueran a desenterrar los animales del cerro. (p.86)

With Tanilo under the ground, a sense of relief enters. The
natural world, absent from the story up to now except as wind,
dust and sun (barring the brief mention of a river) returns, and
with it the sense that the animal and the human are separate. But
if we read this final paragraph carefully, the opposite is also
being implied: the Tanilo they remember is the animal-like,
decaying one who by becoming even more alive to them prevents
them touching each other again. The ending takes us back to the
beginning, and the journey re-starts. Our reading re-enacts the
narrator's process of recognition that the burial is an attempt to
get rid of something that could not be got rid of — that could
not be 'dead and buried'.

Furthermore, the protection of the corpse from animality by
burying it is an acknowledgement of its association with an
animality which cannot be eradicated, just as the sexual taboo
and guilt have to do with the establishment of a safely human
sphere against the encroachments of nature. As the anthropo-
logist Claude Lévi-Strauss has pointed out, the incest taboo is
the first step in the establishment of culture over against nature;
other taboos, such as that against fratricide or leaving the corpse
unburied, play a similar role. Nevertheless, nature cannot fully
be got rid of and always threatens to come back. If Tanilo were
left unburied, the animals would claim him as theirs. Moreover,
as Bataille says in connection with the taboos which surround
death, the cadaver 'testimonia una violencia que no sólo
destruye a un hombre, sino que destruirá a todos los hombres'
(*18*, p.65). It is a threat to the social order as well as to the
individual lives of those who remain. The word Bataille uses is
that the corpse is 'contagious', which would seem to fit the final
description of Tanilo:

> Tal vez los dos tenemos muy cerca el cuerpo de Tanilo,
> tendido en el petate enrollado; lleno por dentro y por fuera
> de un hervidero de moscas azules que zumbaban como si
> fuera un gran ronquido que saliera de la boca de él; de
> aquella boca que no pudo cerrarse a pesar de los esfuerzos
> de Natalia y míos, y que parecía querer respirar todavía sin
> encontrar resuello. De aquel Tanilo a quien ya nada le

dolía, pero que estaba como adolorido, con las manos y los
pies engarruñados y los ojos muy abiertos como mirando
su propia muerte. (p.85)

The swarming flies suggest that he has been taken over by
animality. His brother and wife have not even spoken on the
journey back: the only communication is the sound of flies in
Tanilo's dead mouth which in their memory blots out present
reality. What speaks is animality. He is dead, but he seems alive
with the horror of his own death, in a grotesque parody of the
Christian resurrection of the body. For a moment he becomes a
Christ-figure, with a crown of thorns, but the other two do not
feel pity for him at that moment, only later, when it is too late.
Their human feelings always come too late.

The journey, traditionally a symbol of transformation, has
brought no change, and the narrator is unable to find rest:
'comienzo a sentir como si no hubiéramos llegado a ninguna
parte, que estamos aquí de paso' (p.85). His words echo the
central metaphor of the story, life as a journey to death. The
metaphor is spelt out earlier on, at a key moment. The pilgrims
have converged from all directions, like a river flowing across
the land — a comparison which echoes Jorge Manrique's meditation upon death, especially in the sensation of being subsumed
into something larger than themselves. As they go further, the
desire for change becomes merely the desire to get through the
day to night:

> Algún día llegará la noche. En eso pensábamos. Llegará
> la noche y nos pondremos a descansar. Ahora se trata de
> cruzar el día, de atravesarlo como sea para correr del calor
> y del sol. Después nos detendremos. Después. Lo que
> tenemos que hacer por lo pronto es esfuerzo tras esfuerzo
> para ir de prisa detrás de tantos como nosotros y delante de
> otros muchos. (p.81)

The passage of day to night becomes equivalent to the
movement through life to death, giving a static sense of repeated
time in which nothing changes, just as the guilt does not change.

The inescapability of guilt is predicated on the 'law' of life and death, and the repeated journey, which is never finished but always starting again, is like the repeated movement of the narrator's consciousness from desire to guilt and back to desire.

5. Time: the Presence of the Past

The events of 'Talpa' belong to the sphere of what has already happened and cannot be changed: they can only be re-lived or re-said, but not altered. This type of time-structure, which is that of a majority of the stories, is characteristic of myth. Myths always present themselves as what has already happened and must go on being true, and for this reason they are never traceable to a human author, who would be responsible for them and would locate them in particular time and space. This is similar to the concept of fate, which is derived from the Latin *fatum*, meaning 'that which has been spoken', 'a sentence of the gods', i.e. a reality which cannot be questioned or altered. Although there are identifiable human narrators in Rulfo's stories, their relationship to the events narrated is such that these latter belong to a past which cannot be altered and which dominates the present, erasing any notion of future. This fatalistic type of structure is less the result of personal resignation than of the cultural attitude of a static society, which sees the present as a repetition of the past.

The protagonist of 'Díles que no me maten' is in fact very far from being resigned. Unlike the inhabitants of Luvina, or the people on the pilgrimage to Talpa, he does not accept death: the one thing he will not accept is to be killed for the murder he fully admits having committed. And unlike Esteban in 'En la madrugada', he does not admit any guilt before the law, even though he has even less grounds for defending himself, given that there was no element of self-defence. In fact his attitude does not seem to square with the indifference shown by other characters. This is because what he confronts is not history or the legal system but the more fundamental law (in the meaning given that word in 'Luvina') of revenge, the law which says that, having killed someone, he must pay for it.

The man Juvencio Nava kills is his *compadre*, *compadrazgo* being a closer and stronger bond than the literal meaning, co-godfather, would suggest. In the more traditional (i.e. rural) areas of Latin America, *compadrazgo* is, after the family, the most important social bond. Thus the act of killing a *compadre* is particularly unforgivable. This is not altered by the fact that the cause was a dispute over pasture rights (don Lupe provocatively killed one of Nava's animals) and that as in other stories the murder is thought of by the perpetrator as inevitable and not a matter of personal responsibility: 'tuvo que matar a don Lupe' (p.112). Although he is subject to persecution by the law and loses all his possessions through paying off legal officials, his fear lies at a deeper level. He attempts to reassure himself that he has nothing to fear from the dead man's sons, since they were only babies at the time, but his life is dominated by fear. He moves to as remote an area as possible, but people frighten him with reports of outsiders ('fuereños') in the area, and while he hides in the wilds like a hunted animal, they take advantage and rob him. When four men come to take him away he knows what it is for but is not resigned to dying. Having spent most of his life in fear of death he has not been able to live. His life has been dominated by the time-structure of revenge: because he feared the past would catch up with him, the past has dominated him to the extent that his present existence has become a vacuum. Revenge is precisely a form taken by the past when it becomes present; as Ariel Dorfman puts it, the past is 'encarnado en el vengador'.[3] This is similar to the workings of myth and fate, where the present is something which has already happened.

All of this is underlined by the final part of the story, where it is revealed that the men who came to fetch Nava were sent by one of the dead man's sons, now a Colonel in the army. Nava gives himself away to these *fuereños* by coming down from his hiding place and calling out to them not to tread on the young sprouting corn. It is hope which has betrayed him, the growing corn symbolizing hope for the future. The corn, as he admits to himself, was never going to ripen anyway. Stultified hope is a

[3] Quoted by Marcelo Coddou in *Homenaje a Juan Rulfo*, ed. Helmy F. Giacoman (New York: Las Américas, 1974), p.78.

key theme of the story, and the word *esperanza* is given special prominence. Hope would release Nava from his anxiety: 'No, no podía acostumbrarse a la idea de que lo mataran. Tenía que haber alguna esperanza. En algún lugar podría aún quedar alguna esperanza' (p.115). Hope has strong Christian connotations, and Nava specifically pleads for his life 'por caridad de Dios' (p.111). But Christian compassion and forgiveness are denied, and supplanted by the law of revenge. The Colonel has decided to kill the murderer of his father because 'está aún vivo, alimentando su alma podrida con la ilusión de la vida eterna ... No puedo perdonarle que siga viviendo. No debía haber nacido nunca' (p.117). What he will not allow to Nava is, above all, time.

The operation of the law of revenge can be recognized primarily in the way the details of the first murder, concealed until the end of the narrative, are revealed. Nava has all the time been trying to treat the murder as if it were merely a thing of the past, but the intensity of the details makes it something very much still alive. It is the Colonel who gives the account: 'Luego supe que lo habían matado a machetazos, clavándole después una pica de buey en el estómago. Me contaron que duró más de dos días perdido y que, cuando lo encontraron, tirado en un arroyo, todavía estaba agonizando' (p.117). Although it is recounted by the Colonel, who has tried unsuccessfully to forget, nevertheless we realize at this moment that the killing is something which Nava also has been trying to suppress from consciousness without succeeding. The two characters are brought together by their common inability to forget a past which here comes to life despite the thirty-five years which have elapsed. Nava's own death recalls that of Lupe Terreros, the Colonel's father; in this case also it is the son of the dead man who recounts it: 'Tu nuera y los nietos te extrañarán. Te mirarán a la cara y creerán que no eres tú. Se les afigurará que te ha comido el coyote, cuando te vean con esa cara tan llena de boquetes por tanto tiro de gracia como te dieron' (p.118). The parallels are numerous: the son deprived of a father, the excessive violence, the dead man removed from the family and associated with animality ('pica de buey'; 'coyote'), the total negation of pity or compassion. Each murder reflects the other because the law of revenge demands symmetry.

The important role of time in this story can perhaps best be clarified by considering Blanco Aguinaga's view that the two murders 'son entradas mecánicas y sin sentido del acontecer histórico en la resignación atemporal de la vida de los personajes' (*4*, p.93). The idea is that the characters' state of mind is one of resignation and timelessness and that this timelessness is interrupted by the violent, outside force of history. There are two flaws in his argument. Firstly, Nava is not resigned. Secondly, the timelessness is not simply subjective. Nava's state of mind is anxiety: the one thing he cannot resign himself to is death. The words 'Díles que no me maten', which as well as being the title of the story are uttered by Nava, were painted on a wall in the Universidad Nacional Autónoma de México, the main university in Mexico City, in 1977, at a time when the university, occupied by the students, was being strafed by police helicopters. This helps to show how Nava's anxiety can be read as a response to a society in which the chain of violence does not cease to repeat itself. It also shows how Rulfo's writing has the power to imprint itself on the public memory and to speak in a public space. There can be few writers whose words have the power to become a message on a wall.

Nava had been hoping for chronological time, for more days in his life, but he is haunted by the time-annulling law of revenge. Suppressing the details of the killing is his way of gaining time. The growth of the corn is a mark of time and change, but revenge will not allow change. Thus the fact that he is old, in fact almost dead anyway (his name, suggesting *juventud*, is, like several other names in Rulfo, a grotesque joke) does not make any difference; it does not even matter that he will not be conscious at the moment of facing the shots: revenge is not concerned with learning or experiencing (the Colonel never looks at Nava), only with the crude payment of 'an eye for an eye and a tooth for a tooth', for the sake of which Nava is reduced to a mere symbol. This cancelling-out of time is the product of a static society, which does not believe in legal process as preferable to individual revenge, and whose outlook,

like that of the narrator in 'Talpa' or of the inhabitants of
Luvina, does not allow the possibility of change. It is not
accurate, therefore, to assert that timelessness in Rulfo's stories
is merely subjective. It is a cultural structure which permeates
the subjectivity of the characters and is experienced by them
existentially.

This point can be developed with reference to certain general
characteristics of the stories, in particular their lack of a sense of
future. Let us consider, first, the tendency to collapse chronology. This shows itself in the recurrent doubt as to how much
time has elapsed in a story. In 'Macario', for instance, the first
words are repeated almost exactly some fifteen lines before the
end: 'Ahora estoy junto a la alcantarilla esperando a que salgan
las ranas' (p.92). Since the sense of time passing is produced by
signs of change, the reader is given the sensation that perhaps no
time has passed, that Macario's musing has taken place in a
single moment without extension. There is a similar ambiguity in
'En la madrugada': the beginning and ending refer to dawn, suggesting that everything has occurred within the lapse of a single
day, which is not, however, wholly true — this is the ambiguity
— since Esteban is in jail and telling the events from there. The
time which has elapsed between the events and the telling has
been lost, since it has no significance. Or, in 'El hombre', the
repeated references to the flight of the *chachalacas* produce the
feeling that for Alcancía no time is passing; nevertheless,
whatever he does, time, in the form of revenge, will catch up
with him: this second sense of time is embodied in the smoothly-
flowing river, in which his corpse is finally discovered. Another
feature of this erasure of intervals between one moment of time
and another is pointed to by Blanco Aguinaga, who remarks on
the fact that the characters tend to repeat certain phrases, giving
us the impression that nothing has occurred in between: 'los
personajes de Rulfo tienen la costumbre de recoger, cada cierto
número de frases, la frase inicial de su charla para hacer así que
todas sus palabras queden suspensas en un mismo momento sin
historia' (*4*, p.91). Looked at analytically and conceptually, this
means separating certain moments from the temporal series
(whether of hours, days or years) to which they belong. A

further example, mentioned in Chapter 3, would be the murder of the family as presented in 'El hombre'. Didier Jaén points to a similar process in an essay on the evocative character of Rulfo's style, showing that Rulfo's emphasis is on the time of day or of the year, rather than on which day or which year: 'La insistencia en llevar nuestra atención ... hacia la época del año, hacia un determinado momento u hora del día o de la noche, constituye una de las características más sobresalientes del estilo evocativo de Rulfo' (*21*, p.201). While these features are more pronounced in *Pedro Páramo*, they are also to be found in the stories. The heightened moments of time, because they stand out from the larger chronological series and mirror each other, seem to remove the intervals in between: the beginning and ending of 'En la madrugada' are a case in point. Intense moments become significant, over and above either their extension or their place in a larger chronology.

A further aspect of temporal distortion is the freezing of time at moments of extreme violence, referred to at the end of Chapter 3. The sensation of timelessness, connected with a ritual slowing-down of events, is in fact produced by opposing our sense of normal chronometric time. In Bergson's theory of time, the division of the pure flow of time into separate moments, i.e. into chronology, is a product of the socialization of the self. But this should not make us conclude that Rulfo's characters' refusal of ordinary time is asocial and purely subjective. Bergson's theory refers to modern society, not to a precapitalist society governed by the natural cycles of day and night, the seasons and the stars, a repetitive consciousness of time which Rulfo uses in order to challenge our modern, urban sense of chronometric time.

Not just in 'Díles que no me maten', but in a majority of the stories, the past, through memory, becomes so intensely real that it tends to absorb the present. The period of time elapsed between the occurrence of events and the narrating of them disappears; this is especially so in 'En la madrugada', 'Talpa' and 'Luvina', where it is as if nothing had happened since. In fact nothing has happened: the past has simply continued to repeat itself in the mind of the narrator. And this is because forgetting is impossible. Had either Nava or the Colonel in 'Díles que no me maten' been able to forget there would have been no second murder. As it is, they have both tried to forget and failed. Memory, unrelieved by an ability to forget, breaks down the division between past and present, which points us towards the world of *Pedro Páramo*, where only the past is present.

Because the past, unchanging and unchangeable, is what is most real, there is no sense of future time. As has already been pointed out, fate annuls the future, i.e. the dimension of change. This is reinforced in the fact, dramatized in 'Díles que no me maten', that there is no Christian forgiveness or afterlife. Without the future, the circle of repeated violence cannot be broken. In fact, whatever happens in a Rulfo story, no real change seems to take place. The characters go on journeys, they kill or get killed, but things remain essentially the same. Time does not seem to pass and events continue recurring in a kind of slow-motion after they have happened. The characters appear to picture time in a different way from ourselves. While we think of time as though we were standing in the present, with our face towards the future and the past behind our back, they have their backs to the future and their faces towards the past.

To conclude the discussion of time, it is useful to compare the stories with *Pedro Páramo*, since a number of tendencies inherent in the stories are there taken further and made more visible. In the novel, timelessness becomes literal, to the extent that the characters are all dead, with the present entirely taken over by the ghosts of the past who can find no rest. In terms of narrative structure, different moments of time are juxtaposed, without chronological order, and with no indication at all of intervals. And as in 'Díles que no me maten', the past which takes over the present is dominated by a murdered father, a fact which one inevitably connects with the death of Rulfo's own father.

6. Symbol and Myth

Many critics have pointed out that one of the major character-istics of Rulfo's work is its use of myth. But before considering the presence, in some measure or other, of a wide range of myth-ology, we need to look at how it is brought into the stories. There is no direct articulation, through name or incident, of particular myths. What happens is that there is a fairly constant echoing of symbols and myths, but which despite its frequency is indirect. Angel Rama gives a precise account of this process: 'Sin cesar ... la lectura de Rulfo desencadena juegos analógicos que son especialmente esquivos porque están hechos de alusiones y elusiones, de furtivos rozamientos con grandes y estereotipados mitos' (*15*, p.6). Having established that Rulfo's writing is suffused with mythological echoes, a further issue arises: how far are the myths and symbols in question Greek and Christian, i.e. the ones which are dominant in Western European culture? Carlos Fuentes writes about Rulfo's use of 'los grandes mitos universales', but these all turn out to be Greek ones (*20*, p.16). Augusto Roa Bastos, in an article on *Pedro Páramo*, warns Latin Americans of the danger of being seduced by cultural imperialism: 'He aquí una manera de cautivar los textos: anexarlos sin más a los prestigiosos modelos de la cultura clásica ... Porque la colonización cultural no es sólo imposición sino también fascinación ... Ser dominados culturalmente es ser seducidos' (*26*, p.2). Rama gives a graphic example: 'El peso del pasado, el peso de la historia, el peso del arte, el peso de la dependencia, siguen haciéndonos ver a Hércules en las estrellas' (*15*, p.7). In other words, the dependency of Latin America, on all its levels, both economic and cultural, means that the native American constellations, symbols produced by the traditional native cultures, are not recognized by educated Latin Americans, while they are still remembered, in varying degrees, by rural populations. There is a need, therefore, to place Rulfo's work within a Mexican context. Roa Bastos and Lienhard, in key examples of this type of approach, both stress that the images of hell in *Pedro Páramo*, images which connect closely with the stories, draw on the Nahuatl hell, Mictlan, as much as they do on Greek or Christian notions (*26*, p.3; *22*, pp.476-77).

The limitations of reading the mythical elements in Rulfo in predominantly Greek or Christian terms will be pointed out in more detail below. First, a further problem needs to be considered: in Rulfo we do not find whole myths, or even necessarily whole symbols, but fragments. Rulfo's world is an intersection of the archaic and the modern. A key evocation of the archaic world in modern literature is Baudelaire's sonnet *Correspondances*:

> La Nature est un temple où de vivants piliers
> Laissent parfois sortir de confuses paroles;
> L'homme y passe à travers des forêts de symboles
> Qui l'observent avec des regards familiers.[4]

In this remembrance of the past, nature is sacred and speaks to us, offering forests of symbols. This is the world of animism, where everything in nature has a soul. But the symbols are not fully present, they are echoes, 'Comme de longs échos qui de loin se confondent / Dans une ténébreuse et profonde unité';[5] the lost unity belongs not to our present world, but to a more archaic one, which has been lost. To try to restore that lost unity when reading Rulfo's work is a mistake: if the myths are disarticulated and fragmentary this is because Rulfo's characters do not belong fully to an archaic or a native culture.

'Luvina' may be taken as symptomatic of the cultural processes I have mentioned, as well as serving as an index of how the other stories handle myth. The mythical elements which figure in it are no longer functioning parts of whole cultural

[4] Nature is a temple where living pillars sometimes allow confused words to escape; man passes there through forests of symbols that watch him with familiar glances. (Translated by Anthony Hartley, *The Penguin Book of French Verse*, 3: *The Nineteenth Century* (Harmondsworth: Penguin, 1957), p.155.)

[5] Like long-drawn-out echos mingled far away into a deep and shadowy unity (translated Hartley).

systems. This is the result of the violent discontinuities of Latin-American history, starting with the Conquest and continuing to the present day in the collision of traditional and modern forms of society. What we find are traces and echoes of myths which have been dismantled. As the archaic and the modern confront each other in the story, there is a move from animism to an idea of nature as the representation of personal emotion, an attitude identifiable ultimately with European romanticism.

Let us consider the various interwoven layers which make up the story. The most archaic layer is that of elements of native Mexican culture. Dominant among these is the cult of the dead. The village of Luvina is a type of hell in which the dead are more powerfully present than the living. This is conveyed on various levels. There are the protagonist's and his wife's perceptions: Luvina, when he first sees it, is like 'una corona de muerto' (p.121), i.e. one of the floral offerings made to the dead on All Saints' Day. His wife, whom he sends to reconnoitre, sees only eyes peering from doorways, but nothing that seems human. At dawn, the women of the town appear, sounding and looking like bats. For the inhabitants of Luvina, the dead are alive and dominate their lives: 'nuestros muertos ... viven aquí y no podemos dejarlos solos' (p.127). As Octavio Paz has pointed out, 'para los antiguos mexicanos la oposición entre muerte y vida no era tan absoluta como para nosotros. La vida se prolongaba en la muerte' (*24*, p.49). The dead are treated as if they were constantly present among the living. In a hint or echo of native symbolism, the wires from which hang the crosses in the church sound like teeth as the wind blows on them: these suggest the teeth of skulls, sacred sites full of skulls being one of the features of native culture which most shocked the Spanish conquerors. Wind is a key feature of the story, as will be shown in detail below. To anticipate briefly, wind is an element where native and Christian cultures meet, with the result that the Christian surface of meztizo Mexican culture is stripped away to reveal its native substratum. Near the end of the story, the protagonist warns the inhabitants that the wind will destroy them. They reply, in what is a fragment of archaic cosmology, 'El aire hace que el sol se esté allá arriba' (p.128).

Despite such traces of an earlier cosmology, nature is no longer wholly sacred. Nevertheless, the landscape is perceived anthropomorphically: nightshade plants cling to the ground 'con todas sus manos'; the wild poppy scratches the air; the wind 'rasca como si tuviera uñas' (pp.119, 120). But it is a broken-up anthropomorphism, as if the bodies of the gods which once peopled nature had been shattered, and only vestiges of their presence, like the wind's finger-nails, were left. The protagonist is a schoolteacher, someone who by culture and training belongs to the modern, urban world. He notes the animistic beliefs of the villagers, but cannot relate to them: 'Dicen los de Luvina que de aquellas barrancas suben los sueños; pero yo lo único que vi subir fue el viento' (p.119). For the local people, the wind is a human figure, 'llevando a rastras una cobija negra; pero yo siempre lo que llegué a ver ... fue la imagen del desconsuelo' (p.122). The different attitudes exhibit a move from animism towards a modern view of nature as representing, in images, personal feeling.

Christian symbols, or fragments of them, are pervasive in this as in Rulfo's other stories. They occur here in two main instances: ideas of hell and paradise and the image of the church. Luvina is referred to as a 'lugar endemoniado' (p.123), a term which uses the Christian concept of the devil. The word 'plagado', which occurs in the second sentence, invokes the same semantic area, as does more clearly the notion of 'purgatorio' (p.128). The teacher had originally thought of the village as a paradise ('cielo'), which gives special poignancy to the description, at the end, of the space through which the starlight enters the room as 'el pequeño cielo de la puerta'. The world outside the room where he is drinking has from time to time interrupted the dead and arid atmosphere of his monologue: it is a world of water, greenness and children's play, all of which in Rulfo's universe have paradisal connotations. A fuller working-out of these motifs, which serves to confirm their importance, can be found in *Pedro Páramo*. 'Luvina' is in this sense the story which most resembles the novel. The landscape is that of a failed paradise. Everything, in the opening description of the land, fails to become what it promises:

la tierra de por allí es blanca y brillante como si estuviera
rociada siempre por el rocío del amanecer; aunque esto es
un puro decir, porque en Luvina los días son tan fríos
como las noches y el rocío se cuaja en el cielo antes de que
llegue a caer sobre la tierra. (p.119)

Dampness opposes aridness, but the land of milk and honey
turns into wilderness and the promise of paradise does not reach
the earth.

The dilapidated church where the teacher, his wife and their
children spend their first night is the symbolic centre of the
story. Here the various threads of symbolism are brought
together into a single space. From the Christian side, the church
symbolizes the body of Christ, and thus the redemption of
human beings and the raising of them above death and nature.
However, in this church the altar, the focal point of Christian
ritual, has been dismantled. Etymologically, in Spanish and in
English, to dismantle is to divest of a mantle or cloak, suggesting
stripping away the surface layer of Christian meanings (in a
direct sense, the altar cloth) so as to reveal something else
beneath. It is not said what dismantled the altar, but there is a
strong hint that it was the wind:

Hasta allí llegaba el viento, aunque un poco menos fuerte.
Lo estuvimos oyendo pasar por encima de nosotros, con
sus largos aullidos; lo estuvimos oyendo entrar y salir por
los huecos socavones de las puertas; golpeando con sus
manos de aire las cruces del viacrucis: unas cruces grandes
y duras hechas con palo de mezquite que colgaban de las
paredes a todo lo largo de la iglesia, amarradas con
alambres que rechinaban a cada sacudida del viento como
si fuera un rechinar de dientes. (p.124)

Once again, the Christian symbols are evoked and then dismantled. From a Christian point of view, the wind relates to the
Holy Spirit and the idea of God's message inspiring human
beings. The famous passage in St John (3.8), 'The wind bloweth
where it listeth', is spoken by Jesus in connection with the idea

of rebirth. But the wind in the church of Luvina is more a pagan spirit mixing animal and anthropomorphic qualities. And when it touches the Christian crosses, which are themselves made from local pre-Conquest material, they sound like skulls. Finally, when the wind stops, there is only silence; it is not that it has temporarily effaced the Christian notions of love and hope and that they can return when it stops; they are simply no longer available: 'hubo un momento en esa madrugada en que todo se quedó tranquilo, como si el cielo se hubiera juntado con la tierra' (p.125). The sky has fallen: any Christian notion of heaven has collapsed. The same collapse of Christian symbolism is hinted at in the last image the teacher looks at before he falls asleep: 'Se quedó mirando un punto fijo sobre la mesa donde los comejenes ya sin sus alas rondaban como gusanitos desnudos' (p.128). The conversion of a being with wings into a worm or serpent-like creature has clear Christian connotations and connects with the overall pattern of the collapse of heaven.

There can be no single interpretation of the interweaving strands of symbolism. There is a process of interaction, rather than a single, clear meaning. One of the main sites of interaction is between Christianity and the native death-cult. The church has become a mere shell (of Christian symbols and rituals) filled with a different content. This other content is the animistic figure of the wind and the crosses which sound like skulls. The latter suggest the death-cult which of all aspects of native cultures in Latin America the Christian Church found it most difficult to extirpate. Native beliefs and rituals related to death tend to survive precisely by adopting as an outer shell or protection the Christian symbols and practices which were supposed to replace them. This is the case with *el día de los muertos*, whose outer form is All Saints' Day, but whose dominant image in Mexico is the skull.

Christian elements are, as we have seen, only one strand in this story. On the most general level, there are frequent resonances with what is perhaps the most widespread of all myths, which narrates the death and renewal of life through the yearly cycle of seasons. In this context, the desert-like aridity of Luvina signifies a failure of renewal. The best-known of these myths are the Middle-Eastern ones, in which a male god such as Attis, Osiris, Adonis, or Tammuz dies and is reborn. Such myths tend to include a descent of the god into the underworld, i.e. hell. Does the failure of renewal in 'Luvina' somehow imply that the god has failed to return from the underworld? I have mentioned Middle-Eastern myths, but the Mexican god Quetzalcoatl is much more appropriate to the context and his attributes fit closely with some of the main symbols. Quetzalcoatl is a creator deity, associated with the sun. He initiated the cultivation of maize, conceived as the flesh of human beings, and journeyed to Mictlan, the region of the dead, where he sprinkled the bones with his own blood, turning them into human beings again, hence his attribute of restorer of life. The reason why he fails to restore life in the story is perhaps because he has been permanently banished to the underworld, satanized like many similar native gods by the Christian ideology of the Conquest.

But the key attribute of Quetzalcoatl for 'Luvina' is that he is the god of winds. The animistic figure of the wind is, in part at least, an echo of Quetzalcoatl, and the hands which tear off the altarcloth are, in a sense, his. This level of the story is not its rational or explicit stratum. The wind is the dominant symbol, but it is not a clear symbol which can be interpreted through being traced to a particularly body of mythology. Rather, it is made up of multiple echoes, composite and obscure, but also powerful. It has stripped away all vegetation, leaving bare, barren earth. Here native ideas of hell coincide with the Christian view of the earth as part of the fallen world of nature. Part of its disquieting aspect is that it is a semi-human, animal-like force, which lifts the roofs off houses, scratches walls, and digs its way beneath doors, penetrating everywhere and constantly undermining what culture has built to separate and protect human beings from nature. The animal and the human are amalgamated in the description: 'rasca como si tuviera uñas ... raspando las paredes ... escarbando con su pala picuda por debajo de las puertas' (p.120). It even penetrates within the body, 'como si se pusiera a remover los goznes de nuestros mismos huesos'. Nothing can keep out its primeval force. It is the non-human, the unknown, only partially humanized. In the end, the wind gives way to silence. Is this the silence of Quetzalcoatl, suppressed but not supplanted?

The symbolic conflict between paradise and hell, fertility and sterility is also played out on a perceptual and existential level. The speaker says of Luvina, 'allá viví, allá dejé la vida'; the wind and silence have defeated him: 'eso acaba con uno' (pp.122, 128). It is a place without sensuous qualities. The sky is not blue, but 'desteñido', and so on. Perception of actual sensuous qualities is what defines, psychologically, being in the present. That is what gives intense presentness to those passages where the children are playing. In Luvina, what is real to the senses is the wind, which for the speaker becomes something inward, which he calls 'tristeza' and which eventually becomes silence. Where there is nothing to bring one into present time, 'el tiempo es muy largo', which does not prevent it simultaneously seeming to have been speeded up, as in the image of the head moving up and down to the daily rhythm of the sun: 'Estar sentado en el umbral de la puerta, mirando la salida y la puesta del sol, subiendo y bajando la cabeza, hasta que acaban aflojándose los resortes y entonces todo se queda quieto, sin tiempo, como si se viviera siempre en la eternidad' (p.126). The constantly repeated movement produces a sensation of empty, arid timelessness (in contrast with Christian eternity), occasionally punctuated by the atmosphere of joy and greenness associated with the children. The empty timelessness is something the teacher has brought back with him from Luvina; it has become part of him and shows itself in the way he speaks, 'dando vueltas a una misma idea', as he puts it (p.126). When the sky, with its connotations of paradise, reappears at the end, the man has fallen asleep, as if his consciousness had until that moment been keeping it out, just as earlier on he shoos away the children, telling them to play somewhere else.

The story divides into two sections, the second one beginning with the question, 'Me parece que usted me preguntó cuántos años estuve en Luvina, ¿verdad?' (p.125). The first part of this section functions on a more rational level than what has gone before, introducing biographical and sociological facts in an explanatory manner. The teacher first arrived at Luvina 'cargado de ideas', determined to bring about changes in the isolated rural community in line with his modern ideals, which relate to José Vasconcelos's drive as Minister of Education to move Mexico towards socialism through rural education. The interlocutor to whom he addresses himself and who never answers is going to Luvina and is presumably another teacher who has not yet had the experience of living in an isolated village. The interlocutor, who never answers, has a function similar to that of the reader. Thus the teacher-protagonist mediates between the world of the reader of the stories and the world of the peasantry to which they refer. Where the two worlds intersect, Christian values and rational thinking are undermined. It is also possible to see in the teacher a representation of Rulfo's own experience of returning to his childhood town (see Chapter 2).

In his sociological explanation, the teacher is concerned with answering why the inhabitants of Luvina are unwilling to leave for more fertile land: only old people live there and they have learnt not to believe in Government promises of help. They call their customs 'la ley', thus conferring an unchangeable fixity on their lives. But there is still something mysterious about why they refuse to change or move, a mystery which is one of Rulfo's main motivations as a writer. The sociological stratum comes to a close where rational explanation will not work: people will not leave Luvina because their dead still live there. The only reply the schoolteacher finds is to say that the wind will destroy them, but for them the wind keeps the sun in the sky. We are thus taken back again into the deeper, more obscure strata of the story; the sociological answer is insufficient.

Any disturbing of normal categories has an effect beyond its immediate confines, affecting other relationships also. We have seen how in 'Luvina' the boundary between death and life, normal in modern Western culture, is removed. The same process occurs in other stories, such as when the corpse in 'Talpa' is felt to be alive. The removal of death from everyday life is fairly recent in European culture; in fact pagan rituals addressed to the dead still survive in the remoter rural areas. In Mexican culture, death is not suppressed: as Paz says, 'Para el habitante de Nueva York, París o Londres, la muerte es la palabra que jamás se pronuncia porque quema los labios. El mexicano, en cambio, la frecuenta, la burla, la acaricia, duerme con ella' (*24*, p.52). This can be seen in a number of the stories but nowhere is the almost humorous familiarity with death more apparent than in 'La cuesta de las comadres', where the protagonist demonstrates that one of the Torricos' victims is not alive by kicking him: 'Ya por último le di una última patada al muertito y sonó igual que si se la hubiera dado a un tronco seco' (p.49). Later he talks to Remigio Torrico after killing him: ' "Quisiera que te dieras cabal cuenta ..." Eso le dije al difunto Remigio' (pp.53-54). Once this fundamental boundary between life and death is removed, others tend to shift, particularly those which separate rational and irrational, human and non-human and dream and reality. It is through such shifts that some of the stories' most powerful effects occur.

This chapter would be incomplete without a mention of some of the main groups of symbols in the stories as a whole. It is impossible in the space available to give more than a general outline. The parodies and inversions of Christian symbols, mentioned by many critics, tend to occur, as pointed out earlier, in conjunction with the presence of native cultural elements. Thus in 'Talpa' what starts out as a Christian pilgrimage becomes a grotesque parody, pagan animality subverting the Christian features of the occasion. Sometimes it is the realities of popular rural life, as in 'Anacleto Morones', where humour is directed against Christian piety in terms of a conflict between official belief, which holds that sexuality and religion are mutually exclusive, and actual practice. With 'Nos han dado la tierra', the parody has a political and economic source: the promised land is arid and useless, whereas the land which is green and plentiful is the land which the peasants have not been given because it is too good for them. The last line of the story, 'La tierra que nos han dado está allá arriba', is a parodic reference to heaven as well as a literal reference to the barren high plateau.

Perhaps the most useful way to end would be to outline what

is probably the major cluster of symbols, those that relate to the axis of paradise versus hell, leaving aside at this point the question of whether their origin is Christian or native. For analytical purposes, these symbols can be seen in terms of sets of oppositions, although in practice the opposites do not necessarily occur simultaneously. Thus for example there are frequent images which evoke the idea of paradise but which are not necessarily balanced in their immediate context by others which refer to hell. To trace the patterns is a matter of reading the stories vertically rather than horizontally, much as one can read a musical score vertically, in terms of the harmonies, rather then horizontally, in terms of the melody (which, with a story, would be to read it merely for the narrative line). Paradise is evoked through water, greenness, softness and childhood, hell through aridity, heat, emptiness and lack of air ('Nos han dado la tierra') or sterile wind ('Luvina'). In contrast with the deadness of the non-human animality of hell, paradisal moments include a positive anthropomorphism, where nature is suffused with a gentle tenderness. The following example is from 'El hombre':

> Muy abajo el río corre mullendo sus aguas entre sabinos florecidos; meciendo su espesa corriente en silencio. Camina y da vueltas sobre sí mismo. Va y viene como una serpentina enroscada sobre la tierra verde. No hace ruido. Uno podría dormir allí, junto a él, y alguien oiría la respiración de uno, pero no la del río. La yedra baja desde los altos sabinos y se hunde en el agua, junta sus manos y forma telarañas que el río no deshace en ningún tiempo.
>
> (p.62)

This paragraph interrupts the death-obsessed narrative, introducing a delicate, embracing softness ('mullendo', 'enroscada'). It does not penetrate, invade or efface human beings but gives them a quiet and sustaining space in which to be. It is gentle enough not to break the gossamer-like tendrils of ivy, seen anthropomorphically as hands.

Similar paradisal interruptions occur in 'Luvina', where the flowing river is associated with the playing of children. But childhood is not necessarily positive: when it is orphanhood, as in 'Macario', it amounts to constant fear of purgatory. The world of the dead constantly threatens to engulf the boy. Felipa's milk, 'buena y dulce como la miel que le sale por debajo a las flores del obelisco' (p.92), which echoes the Biblical land of milk and honey, is the only thing that will fill him. Emptiness is a property of that side of the axis which points towards hell. Mother's milk is one of the most powerful symbols in Rulfo, a power which it retains even in old age, opposing the desolation of the old cowherd Esteban's life in 'En la madrugada'. Thus to the list of symbolic attributes of paradise can be added that of mother. The opposition of hell and paradise also emerges in a contrast between different forms of time. The time of hell, whether accelerated or decelerated, is a dead, emptied time, a sterile eternity. Paradisal time is a softly flowing musicality, which holds us gently in the present: 'el sonido del río pasando sus crecidas aguas por las ramas de los camichines; el rumor del aire moviendo suavemente las hojas de los almendros' (p.120).

7. Language

The language which Rulfo has created in his fiction is in many ways his central achievement. Its various facets are best approached in the first place by considering how, within a particular story, the relationship between language and reality is worked out. The most appropriate story for this purpose is 'Es que somos muy pobres', in that it tests the relationship between words and reality, thus providing an insight into the attitude to language in the book as a whole. In the first place, the title is a spoken phrase, a phrase which seeks to explain a situation and by explaining it resolve the conflict between the speaker and the situation. Thus it is a speech act, i.e. about speaking as doing something as well as stating something about reality — in this case, finding a language for things so as to contain the potentially uncontrollable force of nature. The story takes the form of the monologue of a boy working out what it means that the only capital which his family possessed, a cow, has been washed away by the flooded river. It is a monologue in which the usual boundaries between inner and outer speech are absent. As with Macario, communication and meditation, external world and internal world merge. When he speaks about the river he is also talking about something which is inside himself and his family, especially Tacha, but it is not until the end that what he is doing is brought to consciousness.

The situation the boy is confronted with is one where nature, in the shape of the river, invades the human world of culture. Roles are reversed: having broken its banks, the river goes up the street like a person and enters a woman's house. It also invades the boy's sleep, and must, he conjectures, have taken the cow when she was asleep. Emphasis on its invasiveness continues in the stress he places on its smell, since, like sound, smell cannot be prevented from entering the body: 'Se olía, como se huele una quemazón, el olor a podrido del agua revuelta' (p.56). With the idea of burning and rottenness, the river is apprehended as a force which destroys by breaking down and reducing the environment so as to carry it away. When the boy and his sister spend hours watching the river, they are evidently drawn in, fascinated. What are they experiencing? Down by the water they see people's mouths opening and closing, but the noise of the river blots out the voices. The river itself therefore becomes a kind of voice, but as yet what it is saying is not clear: it cannot be contained in words, or not in the words the boy has until then had at his disposal.

The child's inability to rationalize, a feature in greater or lesser degree of all the characters, comes out in the way he uses language. The river has taken his aunt's tamarind tree away 'porque ahora ya no se ve ningún tamarindo' (p.56). He does not understand what is happening — and thus begin to come to terms with it — as a sequence of cause and effect: there is simply the raw fact of the tree's not being there. Similarly, the river is simply 'la cosa aquella' (p.56). Such unanalysed rawness is violent, and difficult to assimilate. A sense of a larger process through which to understand things would have to include a notion of the future, whereby the past would flow through the present to become future. But at this stage of the story the boy is unable to find any future to make sense of the random violence of the present.

The boy and his sister climb the bank so as to hear what people are actually saying, and this is where he hears about the cow being drowned. He imagines how she was caught unawares and failed to save herself. He is now able to see events as a process, to begin to assimilate what is happening. However, there are still things he does not manage to make sense of, such as the fact that his two older sisters became prostitutes. His father's explanation was 'porque éramos muy pobres en mi casa' (p.58). But this explanation, which gives the story its title, does not satisfy him because it leaves unsaid the inner force which drove his sisters to what they did. He then recalls his mother's attempt to explain things in terms of inheritance, an attempt which fails since no-one in her family has been evil. The failure of the parents' explanations is the inadequacy of authority and

tradition, i.e. of culture, to supply a language which can contain
what is occurring.

In the picture of the mouths opening with no sound emerging,
the river destroys language. As it carries things away, it also
takes away their meaning. The cow turns over and sinks, leaving
'ninguna señal de vaca' (p.57); meaning, including meaning
expressed in language, depends on signs: without signs there can
be no meaning — just the meaningless, undifferentiated flood-
water. But the river is also, in a sense, itself a language with
meaning; not inherently, but insofar as the boy, by incorpor-
ating it into his own understanding, makes it into a meaning.
This begins when he takes the imaginative leap of seeing the river
as also something inside Tacha: when she is crying about the loss
of her cow, 'por su cara corren chorretones de agua sucia como
si el río se hubiero metido dentro de ella' (p.59). Then, when he
begins to hear its sound as similar to the sound she is making, its
noise becomes like a spoken utterance: 'de su boca sale un ruido
semejante al que se arrastra por las orillas del río, que la hace
temblar y sacudirse todita' (p.59). There is a hint that the river is
a force inside Tacha, a notion which is consolidated in the final
sentence where her sexuality is perceived as an independent force
— a force of nature — which she cannot control. With this final
step in the boy's reasoning, the river becomes a sign of the
dangerous non-social force within Tacha, a force which the
family are at the mercy of because they are poor. At the end of
the story the title phrase takes on a new meaning and the shape
of the plot can now be recognized as the completion of a thought
which is also the enactment of an utterance. Like the river, the
past flows through the present to the future, and the irrationality
which governs the family's lives is held within a language whose
main symbol is the river. The symbol resolves the contradictions
between nature and culture in that it combines the properties of
both: it is both a meaningless force and a meaningful message.

'Es que somos muy pobres' draws attention to the actual
process of meaning being formed in the contact between people
and their environment and presents it as an issue above all of
sound, of how things are heard. Sound, in linguistic terms, is the
materiality of language, i.e. the material through which

meanings are created and conveyed. The sound-qualities of language are constantly brought to attention by Rulfo through a number of techniques, the most obvious being alliteration, assonance and repeated syllables. These form a constant undercurrent in his prose, and sometimes intensify to become themselves the main focus of attention. Let us consider some initial examples from 'Es que somos muy pobres': 'el agua fría que caía del cielo quemaba aquella cebada amarilla' (p.55), is an instance of assonance (repetition of the *a* sounds) and alliteration (the hard *c* sound). The alliterated consonants mimic the sound of the hard rain destroying the barley. A similarly onomatopeic effect occurs in the final paragraph, where the *r* sounds echo the sound of the river: 'un ruido semejante al que se arrastra por las orillas del río.' Here assonance and alliteration produce a thickening of sound and rhythm; the intensifying effect underlines the major transformation of meaning which is occurring: sound, both in the boy's perceptions and in his words, is the link between Tacha and the river. Rulfo's world is an aural one, where meanings are embedded in sound.

If we consider sound and rhythm in a more general sense, as instances of the foregrounding of sound in Rulfo, the crucial issue is the relationship between sound and meaning, between the semantic and the phonic. This relationship is one of the fundamental resources of poetry and is what gives Rulfo's stories their poetic quality. The following sentence from 'Luvina' is an instance of patterned echoes of sound and meaning: 'Hasta ellos llegaban el sonido del río pasando sus crecidas aguas por las ramas de los camichines' (p.120). The semantic content (the sound of the river) is defined and elaborated by the patterning of vowel sounds *i/o*, *a/a*, *i/a*, which create a sense of the gentle meandering movement of the river. The change from *i/o* to the softer *a/a* and *i/a* conveys the change of feeling when the water is softly touched by the branches. Sound is at least as important here as the semantic content. A sound-picture is produced through the embodying of meaning in the phonic.

In the above example, sound and meaning mirror each other, giving an onomatopeic flavour typical to a greater or lesser

extent of all of Rulfo's language. A more unusual characteristic,
which sets Rulfo apart from other writers, and is almost like a
personal trade-mark, is where both sounds and meanings repeat
themselves, as in expressions like 'el chirriar de las chicharras'
(p.94). This would seem to be a case of simple onomatopeia, but
it is time to consider briefly the implications of this term. Within
the view of language formulated early in the twentieth century
by Ferdinand de Saussure, the connection between the sounds of
words and the ideas they express is always arbitrary and thus
there is never a natural link between sound and object. This is il-
lustrated in the fact that the sound a cicada is supposed to make
differs from one language to another, so that the relationship
between sound and object is always conventional just as words
themselves are conventional signs. However, this theory of a
merely arbitrary connection between the materiality of language
and reality may be said to express a bourgeois, rationalist view
of the world.[6] Rulfo's writing, which draws on other views of
the world, pushes in a different direction.

Let us consider more closely the phrase quoted above ('el chirriar de las chicharras'). There is not merely a correspondence
between sound and meaning but the particular sounds and particular meanings repeat, producing an effect of redundancy. So
much repetition is not necessary to get the meaning across, or
even to create a sound-picture. Something else is involved, which
is not about the conveying of a meaning but about how it is produced, as if it were being said, 'What do *chicharras* do? *Chirriar*', as if the object said itself, spoke itself. The feeling is that
the sound is embedded in the concept (or object) as well as the
concept in the sound. The double embedding occurs in different
degrees, as will be seen from the following examples, which are
arranged in an approximately descending order of overtness of
onomatopeic effect:

el chirriar de las chicharras (p.94)

atragantándose como si se tragara un buche de coraje
                                                           (p.97)

[6] See V.N. Vološinov, *Marxism and the Philosophy of Language* (New York:
Seminar Press, 1973), especially Part II, Chapter I.

chachalacas, graznando con gritos que ensordecían (p.63)

le zarandeaban la cabeza como si fuera una sonaja (p.147)

se quebraba con un crujido de huesos (p.96)

Onomatopeia is not, however, an essential accompaniment of the feature under discussion. There are occasions when sounds and meanings repeat without the sound mimicking the action, as with 'rociada por el rocío' (p.119) or 'asoleándose en el solar' (p.55). These expressions still have the effect of embedding meaning in sound. One of the two *rocí-* stems is redundant — it is there not for concept but for sound: as though the effect of *rociar* were caused in some sense by the sound *rocío*. This produces the sensation that sounds express the properties of nouns rather than being arbitrary. This general anchoring of language via sound in the material world is perhaps a more fundamental feature and the onomatopeic effects a special case of it.

From the equating of sound and substance there follows the notion that sound is not accidental but that it actually does something. The most extreme case is the idea of magical syllables which when uttered in a ritual will have an effect upon the material world. But in a more general sense there is the assumption that words partake of what they refer to. This attitude is typical of oral cultures, where there is a stratum of magical belief and where the magical potency of words is grounded in sound.[7] However, the literary language created by Rulfo is not concerned with a nostalgic return to such forms of culture but involves the creative use of them in order to subvert rationalist views of the world and of language.

Before developing further the subject of orality and oral culture, I shall refer briefly to some of the ways in which Rulfo uses the poetic resources of rhythm and musicality. The variety of rhythms which feature in his prose range between two opposite poles. One of these is a monotonous, repetitive language in which the senses are dulled. The clearest example of this is perhaps the schoolmaster's monologue in 'Luvina'.

[7] Walter J. Ong, *Orality and Literacy* (London: Methuen, 1982), p.32.

Clogged with repeated sounds, this language has a static and colourless feeling to it, as for instance in the first paragraph:

> De los cerros altos del sur, el de Luvina es el más alto y el más pedregoso. Está plagado de esa piedra gris con la que hacen la cal, pero en Luvina no hacen cal con ella ni le sacan ningún provecho. Allí la llaman piedra cruda, y la loma que sube hacia Luvina la nombran cuesta de la Piedra Cruda. (p.119)

Sounds and words repeat in such a way as to prevent any sense of flow or movement, an aspect which is reflected in the lack of any melodic quality. At the opposite pole is a lyrical, evocative type of language, often associated with air and running water, which produces a sense of flowing movement through the melodic play of sounds. If we consider the lyrical passages which interrupt the teacher's monologue, their sensuous vividness depends on a repertoire of musical phrases which repeat either exactly or with slight variations, such as:

el sonido del río (p.120)

el rumor del aire (p.120)

el batallar del río (p.122)

el rumor del aire (p.122)

el chapoteo del río (p.128)

All the lyrical passages in *El llano en llamas* are marked by rhythms similar to these, as indeed are the moments of lyrical intensity in *Pedro Páramo*. There is not space to consider in detail the other rhythmic variations used by Rulfo. They are always embodiments in some sense or other of the action of the story, as for instance in the broken-up rhythms of the opening section of 'No oyes ladrar los perros', which imitate the stumbling walk of the father.

Alliteration is the most frequent device of all in Rulfo's language, a fact which is advertised in the titles of both his books. As well as having onomatopeic and rhythmic functions, alliteration also conveys orality in the most direct sense of the term, which is that speech is of the mouth, by drawing attention to the spokenness of language. When alliterated consonants interrupt the flow of sound we are reminded that words are produced physically by the mouth. In conjunction with this effect, the greater part of the stories are spoken as direct speech rather than narrated indirectly, and all of them have the flavour of spoken rather than written narrative.

Just as speech externalizes the body, through the mouth, so also the environment, converted into words, is internalized through speech. This process is conveyed in the onomatopeic effects. There are also several occasions when a point of break-down is reached because it is no longer possible to humanize the environment through speech. Its non-humanity threatens to invade the person, through the mouth, and to blot out speech. Thus in 'Es que somos muy pobres' the noise of the river drowns the words in people's mouths. In 'Nos han dado la tierra', the heat of the sterile plain dries up the words in the peasants' mouths, just as the State has prevented them speaking, both directly through the Agrarian Reform bureaucrat, and indirectly by giving them the hot, arid land. Their speechlessness is thus a geopolitical metaphor. Finally, 'Talpa' presents speech as the sphere of the human, under constant threat of invasion by animality, as in the image of the dead Tanilo's mouth, full of flies.

In terms of their form of presentation, monologue is very frequent in the stories; 'Macario' is wholly monologue and 'Luvina' very nearly so, while other stories include sections of monologue or approximate to monologue. This is not a psycho-logical trait of the characters in the sense of being an individual characteristic, in other words they are not necessarily 'ensimis-mados' (*4*, p.90). Nor does it mean that when engaged in mono-logue they are not communicating. They listen to themselves speak so as to become, in a sense, interlocutors to themselves. Thought is experienced as inner speech and consciousness as words heard. The fact that thinking is a type of hearing serves to orient the reader towards an attitude of aural apprehension of inwardness and subjectivity. To achieve its full communicative potential, oral language relies on contextual richness: gesture, modulation of voice, etc. Written stories cannot capture this richness directly. But through the complex patterning of sounds and words Rulfo is able to convey some of it indirectly. For instance, the frequent repetitions of whole phrases, which Blanco Aguinaga sees as a sign of the characters' denial of time (*4*, p.91), are in fact a mark of orality. They are instances of the continual back-tracking typical of oral narrative, where the storyteller has to ensure that the hearer is still with him, given that there is no written record to go back to. In order to make sure of the hearer's attention, the oral storyteller punctuates his narrative with frequent references to the current moment of communication. This presence and awareness of the moment of saying features in all of the stories: they all draw attention to the particular moment and circumstance of their telling.

Because grounded in the action of telling, the stories are placed upon a different basis of authority from the impersonality and omniscience characteristic of narrative in the mainstream of the European novel. In 'El hombre' there are two occasions when the prestige of anonymous, written narrative is subtly subverted. At the beginning, there is what seems to be an anonymous and objective description of how Alcancía flees from his pursuer. But at a particular moment the apparent impersonality and non-spokenness is called into question:

El hombre caminó apoyándose en los callos de sus talones, raspando las piedras con las uñas de sus pies, rasguñándose los brazos, deteniéndose en cada horizonte para medir su fin: *"No el mío, sino el de él"*, dijo. Y volvió la cabeza para ver quién había hablado. (p.60)

Alcancía hears the word *fin* as referring to his own death and not to the horizon; when the third-person narrative is heard as a voice, its aura of anonymity and authority is subverted. The convention by which written narrative is allowed an impersonal claim to knowledge is questioned: impersonal utterance does not make sense in an oral culture, since everything is said by someone. Later on there is another interruption of an apparently impersonal piece of narrative: 'Muy abajo el río corre ... No hace ruido. Uno podría dormir allí, junto a él, y alguien oiría la respiración de uno, pero no la del río' (p.62). The introduction of *uno* implies a speaker and a hearer rather than an author and a reader.

Rulfo's stories are not of course completely oral. They are not bound, for instance, by the limitations of oral story-telling which restrict it to conventional treatment of space and time. Their compositional techniques are those of modern, post-Joycean fiction, assembling a world by freely juxtaposing fragments of consciousness rather than aiming to produce naturalistic pictures of life. They combine modern literary techniques with an input from oral culture. This places them, along with José María Arguedas, Roa Bastos and Guimarães Rosa, in one of the most important areas of Latin-American writing, which Angel Rama has called the literature of transculturation (*25*).

Rulfo writes not only about an oral culture but from one. This makes his writing different from that of *indigenismo*, where the cultural code it speaks from is different from the one it refers to. The gap is evident in the fact that in *indigenista* novels the language the characters speak is different from the correct Spanish of the narrative parts.[8] Rulfo's fiction coincides with José María Arguedas's principle of achieving universality through the local itself in all its particularity rather than through adding local colour to a form and style of fiction which arose elsewhere. Describing the culture of highland Jalisco, Meyer, as historian, writes: 'Everything passed by way of the eyes, the ears, and the mouth, and a prodigious vocabulary was possessed by these men commonly regarded as inarticulate ... Their educated contemporaries from the city did not understand one word in three of their beautiful Castilian speech of the fifteenth and sixteenth centuries, the delight of linguists' (*23*, p.182). Rulfo, as writer, speaks in the *Autobiografía* of his decision to 'escribir como se habla', and of his commitment not to 'las voces universales y gloriosas' but 'la voz profunda y oscura' (*1*, pp.55, 62-63).

[8] See Antonio Cornejo Polar, *Literatura y sociedad en el Perú: la novela indigenista* (Lima: Lasontay, 1980).

Conclusions

This study has sought to place Rulfo's stories within their proper historical and cultural context and also to show that they are not merely descriptive or sociological. These two perspectives need not cancel each other out. The stories respond creatively to given conditions, challenging the normal meanings given to them. I have suggested that the reader should resist normalizing the stories by making them more rational than they are. Rulfo takes us into regions of the irrational (such as Macario's hunger) in order to break out of the usual categories imposed on human beings in a modern urban culture. An important aspect of this is his drawing on religious areas of experience, such as trance and ritual, but outside any framework of formal religion. In fact Rulfo's work resists intellectual formalization in general. Instead, it explores the raw collisions of desire and the social apparatus, subverting the normality of the dominant culture. It does not take us into an archaic rural culture for its own sake but in order to engage, on a deep level, with modern readers' location within their own culture. One of the ways it does this is by invoking some of the fundamental myths and symbols of Western culture while refusing the ethical and ideological orders which over time have rationalized those myths and symbols. Thus 'No oyes ladrar los perros' refuses Christian compassion and European confidence in historical continuity, and 'Luvina' constantly echoes Christian symbols while simultaneously parodying them. These, like the other stories, draw on the oral culture of rural Jalisco, with its substratum of precolumbian belief, in resistance to the modern capitalist culture which dominates post-revolutionary Mexico.

The stories generate mystery or obscurity not for its own sake but to heighten awareness of how partial and incomplete our knowledge of self and others inevitably is. What happens in each story is a series of events but also a process of understanding, producing not a complete rational explanation but a realization of the limits of consciousness and knowledge. Thus although at the end of 'En la madrugada' we have an understanding of how Esteban's consciousness works, we do not have a complete explanation of the violence leading to don Justo's death. Nevertheless, the process takes us beyond the immediate confines of the story itself to other areas of silence and darkness, beneath the surface rationality of existence. Like other masters of the short story, such as Anton Chekhov or Julio Cortázar, Rulfo concentrates within a confined space an energy which explodes beyond itself.

I have touched on a large number of issues in the present study, without necessarily developing discussion as thoroughly and extensively as they merit. It is hoped that the reader wishing to pursue any of them further will find sufficient indications and references to provide a basis. Rather than dealing with a few issues exhaustively, I have preferred to open up as many avenues as possible in order to convey as much as possible of the richness and variety of Rulfo's stories.

Bibliographical Note

This bibliography gives a selection of works likely to be most useful in the study of Rulfo's stories. For a more general bibliography, see José Carlos González Boixo, 'Bibliografía de Juan Rulfo', *Cuadernos Hispanoamericanos*, no.421-23 (July-Sept. 1985), 469-90.

EDITIONS

1. Juan Rulfo, *Autobiografía armada* (Buenos Aires: Corregidor, 1973).
2. ——, *El llano en llamas*, ed. Carlos Blanco Aguinaga (Madrid: Cátedra, 1985).
3. ——, *Pedro Páramo* (México: Fondo de Cultura Económica, 1966).

WORKS ON 'EL LLANO EN LLAMAS'

4. Blanco Aguinaga, Carlos, 'Realidad y estilo de Juan Rulfo', in *Nueva novela latinoamericana*, Vol.I, ed. Jorge Lafforgue (Buenos Aires: Paidós, 1972), pp.85-113; also in *La narrativa de Juan Rulfo*, ed. Joseph Sommers (27, pp.88-116). This authoritative and perceptive essay, which situates Rulfo's work both aesthetically and historically, established much of the ground for later criticism.
5. Durán, Manuel, 'Juan Rulfo, cuentista: la verdad casi sospechosa', in *Homenaje a Juan Rulfo*, ed. Helmy F. Giacoman (New York: Las Américas, 1974), pp.111-20. Discussion of the relationship between the stories and *Pedro Páramo*, with particular reference to 'Anacleto Morones'.
6. Foster, David William, 'Rulfo's "Luvina" and Structuring Figures of Diction', in his *Studies in the Contemporary Spanish-American Short Story* (Columbia: University of Missouri Press, 1979), pp.31-38. A structuralist approach to the interplay of speaker and listener.
7. Gordon, Donald K., Los cuentos de Juan Rulfo (Madrid: Playor, 1976). Includes descriptive interpretations of all the stories.
8. Harss, Luis, 'Juan Rulfo, o la pena sin nombre', in his *Los nuestros* (Buenos Aires: Sudamericana, 1966), pp.301-37. Combines useful interview material with valuable critical discussion of a number of stories.
9. ——, 'Rulfo sin orillas', *Revista Iberoamericana*, no.94 (Jan.-March 1976), 87-94. Penetrating study of the ontological role of landscape in Rulfo.

10. Hill, Diane E., 'Integración, desintegración e intensificación en los cuentos de Juan Rulfo', in *Homenaje a Juan Rulfo*, ed. Helmy F. Giacoman (New York: Las Américas, 1974), pp.101-08. Discussion of the role of the reader and of the relationship between character and environment.

11. Kozer, José, 'Relaciones entre el hombre y la naturaleza en Juan Rulfo', *Cuadernos Hispanoamericanos*, no.274 (April 1973), 147-55. Useful and stimulating discussion of the part played by nature in 'Es que somos muy pobres'.

12. Leal, Luis, 'El cuento de ambiente: "Luvina", de Juan Rulfo', in *Homenaje a Juan Rulfo*, ed. Helmy F. Giacoman (New York: Las Américas, 1974), pp.93-98. Detailed commentary on 'Luvina', pointing out its artistic unity.

13. ——, *Juan Rulfo*, Twayne's World Authors Series, no.692 (Boston: Twayne, 1983). General study of Rulfo which includes brief but useful accounts of all the stories.

14. Monsiváis, Carlos, 'Sí, tampoco los muertos retoñan. Desgraciadamente', in *Juan Rulfo: Homenaje Nacional* (México: Instituto Nacional de Bellas Artes, 1980), pp.35-44. Authoritative and very stimulating essay on Rulfo's place in Mexican history and culture.

15. Rama, Angel, 'Una primera lectura de "No oyes ladrar los perros"', *Revista de la Universidad de México*, 29, no.12 (Aug. 1975), 1-8. Very important essay which breaks new ground in the criticism of Rulfo, combining an analysis of the story with a discussion of the place of Rulfo within large-scale cultural patterns. Rama sets out the case for reading Rulfo in terms of Latin American rather than European myths.

16. Rodríguez Alcalá, Hugo, *El arte de Juan Rulfo* (México: Instituto Nacional de Bellas Artes, 1965). Includes descriptive appraisals of 'En la madrugada', 'No oyes ladrar los perros', 'Luvina' and 'El llano en llamas'. The chapter on 'No oyes ladrar los perros' is reproduced in *Homenaje a Juan Rulfo*, ed. Helmy F. Giacoman (New York: Las Américas, 1974), pp.123-33.

17. Sánchez Macgregor, Joaquín, *Rulfo y Barthes* (México: Editorial Domés, 1982). Semiological analysis of 'Nos han dado la tierra'.

GENERAL

18. Bataille, Georges, *El erotismo* (Barcelona: Tusquets, 1979).

19. Fanon, Frantz, *The Wretched of the Earth* (Harmondsworth: Penguin Books, 1967).

20. Fuentes, Carlos, *La nueva novela hispanoamericana* (México: Mortiz, 1969).

21. Jaén, Didier T., 'El sentido lírico de la evocación del pasado en *Pedro Páramo*', in *Homenaje a Juan Rulfo*, ed. Helmy F. Giacoman (New York: Las Américas, 1974), pp.191-205.

22. Lienhard, Martin, 'El sustrato arcaico en *Pedro Páramo*: Quetzalcoatl y Tlaloc', in *Homenaje a Gustav Siebenmann*, ed. José Manuel López de Abiada (Munich: Wilhelm Fink, 1983), I, pp.473-90.

23. Meyer, Jean A., *The Cristero Rebellion: The Mexican People between Church and State, 1926-1929* (Cambridge: University Press, 1976).

24. Paz, Octavio, *El laberinto de la soledad* (México: Fondo de Cultura Económica, 1972).

25. Rama, Angel, *Transculturación narrativa en América Latina* (México: Siglo XXI, 1982), chapters 1 and 2.

26. Roa Bastos, Augusto, 'Los trasterrados de Comala', *Unomásuno* (22 Aug. 1981), pp.2-3. Impassioned assertion of the need to reinstate Rulfo's work within a Latin-American rather than a Europocentric perspective.

27. Sommers, Joseph, *After the Storm: Landmarks of the Modern Mexican Novel* (Albuquerque: University of New Mexico Press, 1968). Includes chapter on *Pedro Páramo* and its place in twentieth-century Mexican fiction.

28. ——, 'Los muertos no tienen tiempo ni espacio (un diálogo con Juan Rulfo)', in *La narrativa de Juan Rulfo: interpretaciones críticas* (México: Secretaría de Educación Pública, 1974), pp.17-22.

CRITICAL GUIDES TO SPANISH TEXTS

Edited by
J.E. Varey and A.D. Deyermond